Joseph Stalin
and Communist Russia

The Yin and the Yang, *an ancient
Chinese figure, is symbolic for
Century Books, since both negative
and positive forces which the figure
represents also shape the lives of
famous world figures.*

*According to folklore, the Yin and
the Yang are present in all things,
functioning together in perpetual
interaction. This balance between
opposing forces, and the influences,
both good and bad, that have molded
the course of history are accurately
portrayed as background material in
Century biographies.*

Joseph Stalin
and
Communist Russia

by Wyatt Blassingame

A CENTURY BOOK

GARRARD PUBLISHING COMPANY

CHAMPAIGN, ILLINOIS

The author and publisher are grateful to Simon and
Schuster, Inc., for permission to reprint verses from
the translation of Evgeny Yevtushenko's poem "Stalin's
Heirs," which appears in *The Rise and Fall of Stalin*
by Robert Payne.

Picture credits:

Bettmann Archive: pp. 33, 47, 52, 59, 105, 150
Photoworld: pp. 42, 70, 88, 126, 144
Sovfoto: pp. 12, 14, 19, 26, 39, 60, 65, 81, 84, 96, 112
    (top), 135, 138, 159, 165, jacket, cover
Tass from Sovfoto: pp. 100, 112 (bottom)

Map by Henri Fluchere

Contents

1. The Land and the Boy

Just south of the Caucasus Mountains, hemmed in on the west by the Black Sea and on the east by the Caspian Sea, lies what is now the Soviet state of Georgia. It is a beautiful land of high, snow-topped mountains and fertile valleys, of much sunshine and clean winds.

Actually a part of Asia, Georgia lies at the point where Asia and Europe merge. Because of its location, invading armies swept back and forth across it for centuries. The Mongol hordes of Ghengis Khan pillaged the land. The soldiers of Tamerlane murdered and burned. Persian and Turkish armies killed the Georgian men and drove the women off like cattle to be sold into harems. Possibly no other part of the world has seen so much cold-blooded horror over so long a period of time.

In 1801 Georgia came under the control of the Russian tsar. Russian power put an end to the tidal flow of invading armies. Indeed, it seemed almost as if history itself had paused; for most of the next century Georgia would remain practically unchanged—Asiatic, remote, wild, and beautiful. Although now ruled by the tsar, it was still in many ways an individual country with a language and people of its own.

It was here in the small town of Gori that Joseph Vissarionovich Djugashvili, who later would be known as Stalin, was born December 21, 1879. His father was a shoemaker, but not a successful one. Perhaps it was this sense of failure that turned him to drink, and the drink that unleashed a violent temper. Three previous children had died shortly after birth, and though this made Joseph particularly precious to his mother, it brought him no affection from his father. Often in a drunken frenzy the shoemaker would beat both his son and wife with anything that was handy. More than once the people of Gori heard Ekaterina, Joseph's mother, wandering the streets at night weeping.

Her son did not weep, even as a child. Many years later a man who had known Joseph when they were both children would say, "Despite those fearful and undeserved beatings, I never heard him cry. Not once."

Instead, he developed a deep, cold hatred not only toward his father, but toward anyone who had power over him. But at the same time he learned carefully to conceal his feelings.

It is easy to understand some of the boy's bitterness. The Djugashvili home was little better than a hovel. It was only about fifteen feet square with a floor of rough brick. It was very dark, as there was only one tiny window. In winter the cold was intense; in summer the heat and smell were almost unbearable. Although the boy's mother worked as a washerwoman and seamstress, there was often little or no food. An acquaintance of those days described Joseph as "a scrawny, sinewy boy with a long face full of freckles and innumerable pockmarks."

The pockmarks were the result of a severe case of smallpox contracted when he was seven years old. At this time he came close to death, but there was more strength in his small, scrawny body than was apparent. Three years later he suffered an even more serious illness. His left arm was injured in some way, and blood poisoning set in. For several weeks the boy lay close to death. Gradually he recovered, but from that time on his left arm was slightly shorter than his right, and he had trouble bending the elbow.

When Joseph was ten or eleven years old, his father died. After this there were no more beatings for the boy, but there was still poverty. His mother made barely enough money to feed herself and her son. However, though many boys from poor families were put to work by the time they were eleven or twelve, Ekaterina was determined to send her son to school no matter what the sacrifice. A deeply religious woman, she wanted Joseph to become a priest. Somehow she got him entered in the local church school.

He was a good student. He enjoyed reading and

Joseph as a schoolboy in the Gori church school

learned quickly. He liked singing in the choir, and both the hymns and the chanting of the priest made a deep impression on him. Years later his articles and speeches, some of them attacking religion, made use of the rhythm and repetition of church liturgy.

At thirteen Joseph read a book that made a profound impression on him. This was a novel with a hero named Koba. Koba was a Georgian who hated the Russian rulers of his native land. He was a man who never forgot or forgave an injury, and he became an outlaw and spent his life wreaking revenge upon the tsar's police.

Vengeance and hatred were two emotions that young Joseph Djugashvili well understood. Koba became his ideal, and some of his playmates called him Koba as a nickname. Some years later when he was living the life of a hunted outlaw, Joseph often called himself Koba to confuse the police.

The church school at Gori had only four or five grades. By the summer of 1894 Joseph had gone as far here as he could. Because his marks were good, his mother was able to get him a scholarship to the seminary at Tiflis, a nearby city. Here he arrived at the age of fourteen, planning to become a priest. But since Tiflis was the most important school in all Georgia, many students who had no interest in religion came here.

At home Joseph's parents had spoken only the Georgian language. Joseph himself, despite his few years

Joseph's mother, Ekaterina Djugashvili

of school, knew very little Russian. All his life he spoke Russian poorly, with a thick Georgian accent. But at the seminary all the teachers were Russian and classes were taught in the Russian language. This angered many of the students who were patriotic Georgians. Teachers had been attacked in the past and one had even been killed by rebellious students.

This spirit of rebellion did not seem to touch Joseph immediately. He studied hard. Books were not easy to get, but he read all he could either borrow or buy. And he not only read, he spent long hours writing poetry, some of which was quite good. His poetry was largely romantic, in praise of nature and his native country. One of his first poems, published shortly after his fifteenth birthday, was called "Morning."

The rose opens her petals
And embraces the violets.
The lily too has awakened.
They bend their heads to the zephyrs.

The lark climbs high in the sky
And sings his ringing song:
The nightingale with subtle voice
Softly sings on:

"Flourish, O adorable country,
Rejoice, O land of Iveria,
And you also, O learned men of Georgia
May you bring joy and happiness to the country!"

There was, however, another side to his character besides that of the young romantic writer of poetry. Years later a man who had been one of his fellow students would say that Joseph had been extremely jealous of his standing in the school. Joseph liked to debate and was very good at it, but if another student did best him in the argument, he turned sullen. He would nurse his grudge for weeks and seek revenge by spreading lies about the person who had bested him.

For two years Joseph's grades and his conduct, so far

as the teachers were concerned, remained good. Apparently he still planned to become a priest. Gradually, however, a change was taking place both in Joseph and in the world around him. More and more people throughout Russia were grumbling about their living conditions and talking about overthrowing the tsar.

At this time Russia had no law-making body such as the American Congress or the British Parliament. The tsar was an absolute monarch who could, and did, pass laws without any advice from the people he ruled. The people themselves were divided largely into three groups. At the top was a small number of nobles who owned most of the land and wealth of the country. Next there was a middle class composed of merchants and professional men such as teachers, doctors, and lawyers, but this was very small.

The vast majority of the people were peasant farmers. Many of these had lived as serfs, belonging to the land and whoever owned it, until the 1860s when serfdom was abolished. Joseph's own parents had been born serfs. Even after emancipation, most peasants remained incredibly poor. Very few could read or write. They stayed on the land because there was nothing else for them to do.

As one of the most backward nations in Europe, Russia had little industry, and in the few factories that did exist, working conditions were extremely bad. True, at this time working conditions in industry were bad all over the world, but they were particularly terrible in Russia. Men were forced to work fourteen and even sixteen hours a day, six days a week, at wages barely above starvation level. Quite naturally the workers grew more and more bitter.

In western Europe industrial workers had long since begun to form Socialist political parties to fight for better working conditions by legal means. Yet it was not until 1893, the year before Joseph entered the seminary, that the first Socialist party of any kind was formed in Georgia, at Tiflis. Its growth was slow. In theory the Socialist appeal was chiefly to men who worked in factories, but there were only a few factories in Tiflis. Actually it was the students at the seminary who became most deeply moved and excited by the new ideas. Better educated than most, they were quick to recognize the injustice of life under the tsar.

Sometime in his third or fourth year at the seminary, Joseph began to take an interest in the Socialist movement. It offered a form of rebellion against authority, and this had an instinctive appeal to him. By 1897 he had joined the Socialist society in Tiflis. Along with other students he began to slip out of the school at night, climbing out of the windows and down the walls to attend the society's meetings. It was at one of these meetings in 1898 that Joseph met his first real revolutionary.

The man's name was Ormozadze. A thin, pale man,

he wore a black blouse and red scarf, a sort of unofficial uniform for revolutionists. He had been exiled to Siberia because of his political beliefs, but had escaped. While Joseph and the others listened, Ormozadze talked about the cruelty of the tsar's police to the political prisoners.

"I have seen prisoners beaten to death with whips," he told them. "I have seen others tied outside a building in the winter and left to freeze to death. And why? What crime had they committed? They had tried to earn a decent living for their families. For that they were tortured and killed."

Ormozadze said the working people of Georgia could not alone overthrow the tsar. Instead, they must combine with the workers from all over Russia, from all over the world. The revolution would not be a war of one nation against another, but of one class against another: the poor against the rulers who kept them poor.

Joseph Djugashvili understood what it meant to be poor. But as he listened to Ormozadze, it was not just the dream of ending poverty that fired his imagination. It was also the dream of revolution, of overturning government and destroying the people who had power over him. Soon he began to slip out of the seminary and spend hours visiting the railroad workers in Tiflis. He told them they must band together, stage strikes, destroy railroad property, and do anything that would cause trouble for the owners and the government.

As Joseph's interest in revolution grew, his interest in school decreased. He almost quit attending classes. Still, the school did not expel him immediately. It was the end of his fifth and last year; he would soon be taking his final examinations and leaving.

Joseph never took the exams. The exact reason is unknown. Later he would say the school expelled him because of his work as a Socialist. The school records show that he was expelled because for "unknown reasons" he had not even attended the examination. His mother would say he had become sick and she had brought him home.

In later years an artist painted this scene of young Joseph as he was expelled from the Tiflis seminary.

Whatever the reason, Joseph's school days came to a sudden end without a diploma.

Many years later Joseph Stalin would tell a biographer that it was his life at the seminary which had made him a revolutionary. "The character of the discipline enraged me," he said. "The place was a hotbed of spying and trickery. At nine in the morning we assembled for tea, and when we returned to our rooms, all the drawers had been searched. And just as they went daily through our papers, they went daily through our souls. I could not stand it; everything infuriated me."

Like many of the statements the adult Stalin made about himself, this one is not completely true since he would have probably become a revolutionary anyway. But the truly strange thing about it is this: When Stalin made the statement, he himself had adopted the very methods about which he complained. He had turned not just a seminary, but all Russia, into a land where children spied on their parents and neighbors spied on neighbors, where the secret police not only went through the papers of the people, but daily destroyed their souls through privation and terror.

2. Riots and Revolutions, Prisons and Escapes

Joseph was nineteen years old when he left the seminary; probably he had no definite plans about what he wanted to do. But certainly he no longer wanted to be a priest. He had already made contact with the Socialist underground, and for him the work of a professional revolutionary had a deep appeal.

For many years there had been small numbers of men, not only in Russia but throughout Europe, who dedicated themselves to the overthrow of capitalist governments and to the establishment of Socialist or Communist states though none of them had yet succeeded. By far the most important of these had been a German scholar and philosopher named Karl Marx. In 1848 Marx and Friedrich Engels, another German, had published the *Communist Manifesto,* a short book that called for a revolution by industrial workers. Although Marx himself had died only a few years after Joseph Djugashvili's birth, his books continued to be studied throughout the world.

Even so, in Russia the word "communism" was not much used during Joseph's youth. Instead, members of the small political parties that worked to overturn the tsar's government were usually called Socialists. Later a tremendous difference would develop between socialism and communism, with communism by far the more radical of the two. But until the Russian Revolution of 1917, the two words were often used to mean the same thing.

Under the capitalist system the land, factories, and businesses—"the means of production"—belonged chiefly to individuals. Under communism these means of production would belong not to individuals, but to the nation as a whole. Theoretically, then, profits would be shared equally by all the people. There would be no rich and no poor in such a country. Human greed might not be abolished, but the means of profiting by it would be. Every man would work "according to his ability" and in turn be supplied with money and goods "according to his need," the *Communist Manifesto* said. Indeed, once such a way of life was well established, according to Marx's and Engels' theory, there would no longer be any need for government—the government would "wither away" leaving every man completely free.

It was a wonderful dream, and many men believed in it with all their hearts. To them capitalism was essentially evil, and they were sure socialism would create an ideal world in which all men were truly equal. Some of them believed that to establish such a government, a revolution would first be necessary. The idealistic revolutionary was willing to sacrifice his life for such a dream.

Joseph Djugashvili, however, was never an idealist. Ideals and theories never had any deep appeal for him. He found it far easier to be *against* than *for*. He could sympathize with the poor, but he had no burning passion to help them. Probably the basic passion that led Joseph to become a revolutionary was hatred for those in power.

Whatever the motive that drove him, neither Joseph nor anyone else could have been a professional revolutionary without an intense dedication to the cause. The life was both difficult and dangerous. The Socialist parties (there were several) were poorly organized. Many of the leaders were in exile. There was little money, and workers like Joseph went for long periods without any pay at all, and with little at best. Hunted by the police, using different names to avoid arrest, the revolutionaries kept moving from one hiding place to another.

This type of life quite naturally made the keeping of any records difficult or impossible. Even today there are many periods in the life of Joseph Stalin about which we can only guess.

After he was expelled from the Tiflis seminary in 1899, Joseph may have gone home to Gori. By the end of that year, however, he was back in Tiflis and had a job as a clerk at the local observatory.

It was only a part-time job, but it gave him a room,

a small salary, and time to work with the Socialist group he had joined while still in school. Along with them he passed crudely printed pamphlets to the railroad and factory workers. He helped organize discussion groups. Many of the Tiflis workmen were completely illiterate, and Joseph Djugashvili with almost nine years of school seemed highly educated to them. They listened while he talked about their terrible working conditions, their lack of pay, and poor housing. Joseph was never a good public speaker; his voice had a grating edge. But since working conditions were actually as bad as he described them, the men listened and were moved.

One of Joseph's activities was to write articles for an underground revolutionary newspaper. In these articles his use of rhythm and repetition clearly showed the effect of his early religious training. The things he had to say showed even more clearly what he was now thinking.

> Not only the working class has been groaning under the yoke of Tsardom . . . Groaning is the hunger-swollen Russian peasantry . . . Groaning are the small town-dwellers . . . Groaning too is the lower and even middle *bourgeoisie* that cannot put up with the tsarist knout and bludgeon. . . .

The groans of the Russian *bourgeoisie* (the middle

class) did not, however, make Joseph Djugashvili feel much sympathy for them. He quickly added that the bourgeoisie "know only too well how to stir a fire with other people's hands," and that all they wanted was for the poor "to pick their chestnuts out of the fire" for them. If a revolution came, Joseph wrote, it would have to be led by the proletariat, as the Socialists called the working class.

Joseph had been at his job in Tiflis about a year and a half when the workmen staged a demonstration to demand better wages and hours. Some 2,000 strong, waving red flags, they began a march through the city square.

As they marched, one man noticed that the worker next to him was wearing a fur hat and a heavy winter coat although the weather was hot. "Are you sick?" he asked.

The man in the fur coat grinned. "I'm perfectly well."

"Then why in the world are you dressed like that?"

"It was young Djugashvili's idea. If the mounted police ride into us with their whips, the coat and hat will soften the blows." He laughed. "That boy is a pretty crafty character. He plans ahead."

Later Joseph wrote an article telling how he and other revolutionaries in Tiflis had incited the workmen to stage this march. In the article he said that he had hoped women and children would become involved, because

This early photograph of the young revolutionary Joseph Djugashvili was in the files of the Russian police.

if they were injured or killed by the police, it would create more bitterness than if men only were involved.

As it turned out, the marching column was composed only of workmen when, suddenly, it came face-to-face with a wall of police. An officer with a megaphone shouted, "Halt! Stop where you are!"

The line of marching workers wavered. The men crowded against one another and stopped.

"Break up!" the officer shouted. "Return to your homes."

Back in the crowd of workers someone threw a rock. Then another, and another. With a cry the police charged, swinging their swords. From side streets mounted police wielding whips rode into the crowd. The marchers broke and fled, but behind them they left fourteen badly wounded men. Fifteen others were arrested by the police.

And Joseph? He would say later that he had placed himself at the head of the marchers "like a banner." If so, apparently no one saw him there. He was neither wounded nor arrested, and the chances are he was not at the front of the column, but somewhere in the back or on the side, urging the men on. He probably had decided that there were plenty of men who would march at the head of the parade and get shot or arrested, but only a few who could arrange the demonstration in the first place and persuade the workmen to take part.

After two years with the Tiflis Socialists, Joseph moved to Batum, a city on the Black Sea. Here he worked with another Socialist group to organize the workers. By now he was using a variety of nicknames in order to confuse the police, and the alias he used most often was Koba, the name of the fictional outlaw he had admired so much as a youngster. For the next several years Joseph would be best known as Koba.

As Koba, he had been in Batum several months when the workers in one of the factories went on strike. The government immediately arrested a number of the strike leaders. Next day nearly all the workers in the city struck. In orderly ranks, unarmed, they began a march through the city toward the office of the military governor. In the lead were two workmen who had been selected to ask for the release of the arrested strikers.

This time the marchers were stopped by a troop of soldiers. There was some argument, rocks began to fly, and the soldiers opened fire. When it was over, fourteen of the workers were dead, fifty-four wounded, and more than five hundred had been arrested.

Whether Joseph stood "like a target" at the front of the marchers, as he later claimed, or moved along the edge, he escaped without injury. By now, however, his work was becoming well known to the tsar's secret police. A few days after the Batum massacre, he was arrested.

Justice under Tsar Nicholas II worked slowly, if at all. For more than a year Joseph was simply held in jail while the authorities decided what to do.

During this time, in the summer of 1903, a group of Russian Marxists held a meeting. Since many had been exiled from Russia, the meeting was held in western Europe—in Brussels and later in London. The purpose was to unite all Russian Socialists into one party, but instead the delegates wrangled and fought among themselves. Eventually they did agree to call themselves the Russian Social Democratic Workers' party. Immediately, however, this party split in two parts: Members of the more radical group were called Bolsheviks, which meant they were the majority; members of the more moderate group were called Mensheviks, or the minority. Vladimir Ilyich Ulyanov, who under the name of Lenin would become one of the most revered leaders of world communism, headed the Bolsheviks.

This London meeting would affect not only Joseph's life, but also world history. At the time, however, sitting in a Russian jail, Joseph knew little about it. Just as the London meeting broke up, he was taken out of jail, sentenced to three years in exile, and sent to Siberia.

Siberia is the tremendous territory of northeastern Russia, an area as large as the forty-eight contiguous states of the United States. In 1903 it was a land with few cities; even the villages were scores of miles apart, connected by dirt roads that were often little better than trails. Much of the country is covered by vast forests, lakes, and rivers. Winter temperatures in some areas are the coldest on the face of the globe.

It was here that for many years the Russian tsars sent their political prisoners. Once here, they were not confined in a jail but merely required to stay in a general area. A policeman was supposed to check now and then to make sure the prisoner was still there, but actually there was almost no supervision.

The area to which Joseph was sent was not as remote as much of the country, so he had been there only a few weeks when he set out to escape. According to his own story, he simply started to walk away, carrying a rifle that had been given to him. It was early winter, but already snow covered the ground. Before he had gone far, wolves began to follow him. He shot several, but for each one he killed, two new ones appeared. Gradually the wolves began to close in upon him.

Darkness was gathering. The temperature had dropped far below zero. There was no place to rest, and he dared not stop with the wolves around him. At last he turned and began to retrace his steps. Hours later, stumbling through the darkness, almost frozen, he reached the cottage from which he had set out.

A few days later when a break in the weather occurred, Joseph set out once more. This time, apparently without any serious problems, he used a sleigh to reach a more civilized area, then took a train, and returned to the Caucasus.

It was about this time that Joseph married his first wife. Very little is known about her except that her name was Ekaterina Svanidze. She was a peasant girl, deeply religious, like Joseph's mother, and not too bright. And in his own way, Joseph seemed to have loved her. They had a son named Jacob.

After his marriage, Joseph continued his work as a Marxist revolutionary. He wrote articles for underground newspapers and helped organize strikes. However, much of what he did at this time is still unknown. Even years later, rewriting his own history to make it seem important, Stalin left these years largely blank.

At this time the rest of the country was in a growing ferment. Everywhere discontented people were asking, as loudly as they dared, for better living conditions and more liberty. The crisis came on January 22, 1905.

In St. Petersburg some 200,000 workers gathered on a Sunday morning. Peaceful, unarmed, led not by revolutionaries, but by a priest named George Gapon, they marched toward the tsar's Winter Palace. The vast majority of the crowd believed sincerely that the tsar —the Little Father as they called him—was truly a friend of the people. The lack of liberty and the horrible working conditions, the people thought, were caused by the tsar's advisers, and if they could only explain to the tsar, everything would be made right. With them the marchers carried a petition which began:

> Sire: We, workers and dwellers in St. Petersburg, have come to thee, Sire, with our wives, daughters, and helpless old parents to seek truth and protection. We have become beggars; we have been oppressed; we are weighted down with unbearable toil; we have suffered humiliations . . .

The head of the marching column reached the square

in front of the Winter Palace. The rest of the column wound backward for many blocks. Suddenly soldiers appeared from all sides. Moments later came the crash of gunfire. At almost point-blank range troops shot down the marchers. One witness reported that "little boys who had climbed the trees to watch what was going on were shot down like birds." There would never be any accurate count of how many persons were killed and injured. Estimates ran from 150 dead and 200 wounded to more than 1,000 killed and 3,000 injured. The day on which this massacre took place came to be known as "Bloody Sunday."

A wave of horror and indignation swept across all Russia. Most of the army was still loyal to the tsar, so at first there could be little open rebellion, but all across the country people began to go on strikes. These were not only factory workers, but students, professors, doctors, and lawyers. Entire cities closed down; the work of a nation came to a halt.

In St. Petersburg, the capital, and then in other cities, various groups of strikers elected councils to speak for them. These councils were called soviets, which simply meant councils or commissions. In some places, particularly in St. Petersburg, these soviets were for a while almost as important as the tsar's government.

At this same time Russia was in the midst of a very unpopular war with Japan. Now with his people in revolt at home, even Tsar Nicholas finally admitted something needed to be done. Promises were made that the people could elect a *Duma*, somewhat similar to the United States Congress, and the nation would have more self-government than ever before.

For a while it seemed as if the 1905 Revolution had been a success. But almost immediately after the rebellion died down, Nicholas and his advisers began to backtrack on their promises. The Duma actually had very little power because the tsar could dissolve it at any

In the aftermath of Bloody Sunday, uprisings took place throughout Russia. This painting shows workers fighting in the streets behind a barricade.

time if he did not approve of the laws it passed. Men who had played leading parts in the rebellion, moreover, were arrested, executed, or sent into exile.

While all this was going on, the Bolshevik faction of the Social Democratic Workers' party held a meeting. Joseph had become a Bolshevik, probably because it was the tougher, more radical division of the party. Now he was one of the delegates, and it was at this meeting that he saw Lenin for the first time. Years later he wrote:

> I was expecting to see the mountain eagle of our party, a great man, not only politically, but if you will, physically, for I had formed for myself an image of Lenin as a giant, stately and imposing. What was my disappointment when I saw the most ordinary looking man, below middle height, distinguished from ordinary mortals by nothing, literally nothing.

If Joseph was not impressed by Lenin's looks, Lenin was even less impressed by Koba, as Joseph was still called, barely noticing him, if at all.

After the meeting Joseph returned to Georgia. The tsar's repressions were growing ever worse, and Joseph was often in hiding under assumed names.

Then in the spring of 1907 his wife died. She was

still young, and we do not know why or how she died, but a boyhood friend later wrote about the funeral:

> When the modest procession came to the cemetery gate, Koba [Joseph] firmly pressed my hand, pointed to the coffin and said, "Soso, this creature softened my stony heart. She is dead and with her have died my last warm feelings for all human beings."

> From the day he buried his wife he indeed lost the last vestige of human feeling. His heart filled with the unutterably malicious hatred which his cruel father had already begun to engender in him while he was still a child. . . . Ruthless with himself, he became ruthless with all people.

We do not know what was done with the child Jacob Djugashvili at this time. Probably he was sent to live with grandparents. At least he disappeared from his father's life for many years. Meanwhile, Joseph returned to his work with the Bolshevik party.

Even a Communist revolution requires money. Guns must be bought; newspapers and magazines must be published for propaganda. Revolutionary workers, men like Joseph and Lenin, must have money enough for food and clothing. Since few of the revolutionaries had money, they set out to get it by what seemed the most direct method.

This was simple robbery, though the Bolsheviks referred to it by the more flowery name of "expropriation." At the point of a gun they expropriated money from banks, railroads, businesses, and individuals. The idea was Lenin's, who could be as ruthless as Joseph when necessary, and it marks a basic flaw in the theory of communism, as interpreted by Lenin. Under this theory, if the end to be gained is desirable, then any means, no matter how cruel or vicious, are permissible to reach this end. Lenin saw communism as an end that would better the life of the average man, and so robbery, murder, or any method that would help reach this end should be used.

The most dramatic of all the expropriations staged by the Bolsheviks took place in Tiflis not long after the death of Joseph's first wife. A tremendous amount of money was to arrive in Tiflis by mail. From the post office it would be transferred to the bank in a carriage surrounded by eighteen mounted police. Joseph and other Bolsheviks knew this and laid careful plans.

As the carriage carrying the money reached one of the city squares, bombs suddenly began to burst around it. Horses screamed and plunged. The wheels were blown from the carriage. More than fifty persons, most of them innocent passersby, lay dead or wounded. In the wild confusion a man ran to the wrecked carriage, grabbed the bags of money, and began to race away.

Suddenly another man in the uniform of a police officer appeared in a second carriage. Waving a pistol, he rode alongside the running man. "You are under arrest!" he shouted. "Get in this carriage, or I'll fire!" The man carrying the money climbed into the carriage. Then it drove off and disappeared.

Later the tsar's police learned that the man in the officer's uniform was an almost legendary Bolshevik outlaw named Kamo. He was a friend and associate of Joseph, but what part Joseph played in the Tiflis expropriation is still uncertain. The police could never prove anything against him. But it is believed that he helped draw up the plans.

Although nothing was proved against Joseph in connection with the Tiflis robbery, he was arrested a year later for helping organize a strike in the city of Baku. Once more he was sent to Siberia, and once more he escaped almost immediately.

For the next few years Joseph's life was a series of arrests followed by trips to Siberia, then quick and easy escapes. Today many people believe that at this point he was actually leading a double life—working not only as a Bolshevik revolutionary, but also as a spy for the

The exiled Stalin lived in this cabin in Siberia in the years just preceding the Russian Revolution.

Russian secret police. If so, this may explain why time after time he was sent to a part of Siberia from which escape was relatively simple. There is, however, no proof one way or the other.

It was about 1912 or 1913 that Joseph Djugashvili first began to use the name Stalin, which means "man of steel." Years later he told a biographer the name had been given to him by friends "because they thought it fit." More likely it was Joseph himself who thought it fit and chose it for himself.

It was under the name Stalin, or sometimes Koba, that he began to work as an editor of a Socialist newspaper in St. Petersburg. Gradually he was becoming better known in the Bolshevik party. In 1912 he was appointed to its Central Committee, and several times he was sent abroad to attend conferences. At these he came to know Lenin better, and Lenin sometimes helped him write political articles.

Then in 1913 Stalin was arrested once more. By now he had almost certainly broken with the tsar's police, if he had ever actually worked for them. This time he was sent to a part of Siberia that lay very close to the Arctic Circle. From here escape was almost impossible.

Many revolutionaries spent their time in exile studying and writing articles. Stalin seems to have spent most of his time fishing and trapping wild animals. He settled down almost as if he were going to spend the rest of his life there.

But far off in Europe, World War I had begun in 1914. The armies of the tsar suffered terrible losses. One defeat followed another. And all across Russia the seeds of revolution continued to sprout.

3. The Revolution of 1917

As World War I continued, the Russian army suffered such heavy losses that the tsar ordered drafting not only of older men, but even of political prisoners. So it was that in December 1916 Joseph Stalin received orders to report to the military authorities in the city of Krasnoyarsk. The journey, sometimes on foot, sometimes in a sleigh drawn by reindeer, took six weeks. Then the army doctor took one look at Stalin's crippled left arm and shrugged. "You are no good for the army."

For some reason Stalin was not sent back to the Arctic, but to a small Siberian town called Achinsk. There were other political prisoners here, and from them Stalin learned something of what had been taking place in the world while he hunted and fished.

Russia had entered World War I as an ally of England and France, but for the Allies the early days of the war had not gone well. This was particularly true for Russia. Whole divisions of the tsar's army had been sent into combat without sufficient food or clothing, sometimes without arms. Men had been slaughtered by the thousands and tens of thousands. Although the country as a whole still produced enough food, transportation had broken down in many places. Rich men stored away great supplies of food, and the poor, particularly in the cities, went hungry.

But starvation had always been common in Russia. In the little town of Achinsk, Stalin had no way of knowing the rest of the story.

Tsar Nicholas II was not only weak, but incompetent. As conditions in Russia went from bad to worse, even the nobility began to wish for a change. In the army, officers as well as privates were sick of the way the war was being fought. From one end of the country to another, people seethed with unrest.

In the nation's capital of Petrograd (the name had been changed from St. Petersburg), workers began to go on strike. Day after day more people crowded into the streets, chanting, "Bread! Bread!" The tsar ordered troops to break up the crowds. There was some firing; people were killed in the streets, but the crowds grew bigger. On Sunday, March 11, 1917, one regiment of soldiers refused to fire on the people. Instead, it joined with them, marching and shouting for "bread!"

Next day came the explosion. Crowds turned suddenly, violently, into wild mobs. They stormed into prisons, killing the guards and releasing the prisoners. They poured into government buildings, destroying furniture, windows, and anything else they could break.

Soldiers, ordered to fire on the mob, joined the mob instead. By nightfall no government of any kind existed in Petrograd.

From the capital the revolution spread swiftly to other cities. The tsar was forced to abdicate. Officials who had been appointed by the tsar were killed or went into hiding. Within the space of a few days, the government of tsarist Russia simply vanished.

In Achinsk, Stalin and the other political exiles could only stare at one another. Some of them had spent

Russian soldiers and the people of Petrograd raise the red flags of revolution in front of the Winter Palace, home of the tsar and his family.

their lives working and planning for a revolution. Now the revolution had taken place and not a single Bolshevik, Menshevik, or Social Revolutionary had played an important role. Instead it had been a revolution of the people, a simple explosion without any plan at all.

Years later Lenin, Leon Trotsky, and Joseph Stalin would be regarded as the giant figures of the Russian Revolution. But in those wild days of early March 1917, Lenin was in Switzerland, Trotsky in the United States, and Stalin in exile in Siberia.

Although Stalin played no role in the March explosion, he was quick to take advantage of it. There were no longer any police to keep him in Achinsk. A telegram was sent to Lenin that read: "Fraternal greetings. Starting today for Petrograd." It was signed by Stalin and two other Bolsheviks: Lev Borisovich Kamenev and Matvei Muranov.

Stalin arrived in Petrograd to find a city gone mad with joy. After centuries under the oppressive rule of the tsars the people were free, and in their happiness they felt sure that liberty would last forever.

No one paid much attention to Stalin's arrival in the Russian capital. His name was still not well known, except to a few leaders of the Bolshevik party. But now he and Lev Borisovich Kamenev found themselves the highest ranking Bolsheviks in Petrograd, and together they took over the editorship of *Pravda*, the party newspaper.

At this time what little governmental power existed in Petrograd was divided between two groups. One of these, called the Provisional Government, was composed of men appointed by the old Duma, which itself had been without any real power. Some members wanted to reestablish a monarchy; some wanted a truly democratic government; some were not sure what they wanted. Whatever they wanted, they had no way to enforce it. There were no longer any police. Part of the army still fought against the Germans at the front, but the soldiers in Petrograd were as likely to use their guns to rob a store as they were to obey orders, no matter where the orders came from.

The second group that offered some form of government was the soviets. Similar to those that had been organized during the 1905 Revolution, these were councils whose members came from factories and workshops, from the army and navy, and from almost all the groups of Russian workers. They formed a huge, unwieldy mass whose only real power lay in the fact they represented so many of the Russian people.

No nation can exist without a government able to enforce its laws. Russia was headed toward chaos. The wild joy of the people at the overthrow of the tsar was soon tempered by fear of total anarchy and lawlessness.

As the most prominent Bolsheviks in the capital, it was up to Stalin and Kamenev to decide what form of government their faction of the party would work to establish. The two men talked it over. They could co-operate with the Provisional Government, or with the soviets. Or they could come out against both and attempt to establish a government dominated by the Bolsheviks.

Kamenev was essentially a mild man. He had worked for revolution because he wanted a government representative of the people. Now that a revolution had taken place, he was willing to work with other factions to bring order out of chaos.

Cautiously Stalin agreed, though his reasons were somewhat different. By nature he was both tougher and more radical than Kamenev, but he was also more inclined to be careful. He was thirty-seven years old; never in the past, however, had it been his job to make important policy. Most of the earlier editorials he had written had merely repeated the arguments originated by Lenin and other Bolshevik leaders. He had no original ideas about the type of government he would like to create. Also he knew the Bolsheviks were only a small minority of the Russian people, and he did not believe there was any chance for the Bolsheviks to take power. It was his nature to be cautious and to stay in the background until he knew which way the wind blew. So now Stalin wrote editorials suggesting that the Bolsheviks cooperate with both the Provisional Government and the soviets, at least for a while.

In Switzerland Lenin, the recognized leader of the Bolsheviks, read these editorials and grew furious. To him what had occurred in Russia was only half a revolution. The monarchy had been overthrown, but not capitalism. Although the men of the Provisional Government were great liberals if judged by the standards of the tsar, they were conservatives and reactionaries according to Lenin's standards. And Lenin was a man who did not doubt his own rightness; he was absolutely sure of his ability to run the government, if he could only get his hands on it. He almost exploded with impatience to return to Petrograd.

Transportation was difficult between these two countries, because Russia was still at war with Germany. But the German government, having decided that whatever Lenin did was more likely to hurt the Allies than to help them, allowed him to cross the country in a sealed train. On April 16, 1917 he reached Petrograd. Next day he addressed a meeting of some 200 of the Bolshevik party leaders, including Stalin. The things he had to say shook them like thunder.

"What kind of a revolution," Lenin demanded, "is this that allows capitalists still to control our country? Why has the party developed no plan to take com-

Lenin speaking at an outdoor meeting in Moscow
soon after his return from exile

mand?" Well, Lenin said, he had a plan, and promptly
he outlined what would be known in history as the
"April Theses."

The Bolsheviks, Lenin said, must not cooperate with
the Provisional Government because this government
would never approve of socialism. Instead the Bolsheviks
must do everything possible to destroy the Provisional
Government.

Since the Provisional Government and the soviets
were now competing for power, the Bolsheviks would,
for a short time, help the soviets. However, their main

purpose should be to elect party members to the soviets so that later these groups could be taken over by the Bolsheviks.

The war with Germany, Lenin said, must be ended. But "... it is impossible to end the war ... without the overthrow of capitalism." The Allies were capitalist nations, and it was the destruction of world capitalism toward which the party must aim. For that reason no parliamentary republic must be allowed in Russia. Therefore, the army and the police, which upheld the present government, must be disbanded.

Moreover, Lenin continued, the private ownership of land must be abolished.

Lenin did not mention Stalin by name, but he tore into the editorials that had appeared in *Pravda*. Some of them were "nonsense ... flagrant mockery ... a fog of deception."

The Bolsheviks, Lenin said, were the only group tough enough to lead a world revolution. Therefore they must break with all other Socialist groups. To make this clear they should no longer call themselves Social Democrats, but Communists. (As time went on, the names Bolshevik and Communist came to be used interchangeably.)

For two hours Lenin spoke without pause. He was a small man with a high domed forehead, high cheekbones, and a pointed beard—nothing much to look at.

But by the sheer, electrical force of his personality, he changed the course of Bolshevism and with it the history of Russia and of the whole world. Later a Russian journalist named N. Sukhanov who had been present wrote that when Lenin spoke "it seemed as if all the elements had been let loose from their depths and the spirit of All-Destruction was sweeping through the hall. . . . I went out into the street and had the feeling of having been beaten on the head all night with chains."

Not all the Old Bolsheviks agreed with Lenin at first. Kamenev strongly defended the editorials he had written asking for support of the Provisional Government. But Kamenev admired Lenin tremendously, and gradually he was won over.

Stalin's course was typical. He did not defend his views, neither did he suddenly change them. Instead, he retired into the background; he seemed almost to vanish while he watched and waited to learn which way the Bolsheviks would go.

The Bolsheviks went with Lenin. His boldness, his self-assurance, and his undoubted brilliance furnished an inspired leadership that they could not resist. Also, Lenin's plan to destroy completely the old social system was one that appealed to Stalin. Within ten days after Lenin's speech, Stalin was writing editorials agreeing with it, even when they flatly contradicted things he had written previously.

Before Lenin's return, Stalin had written that the peasants should not take land by force from its former owners. Now he wrote they should take justice in their own hands, seize the land "without waiting for any permission." Whereas before he had said that he doubted workers in other countries would join the revolution, he now wrote: "Under the thunder of the Russian Revolution the workers in the West, too, rise from their slumber. . . . The ground is burning under the feet of the capitalist robbers—the Red banner of the International is rising again over Europe."

For all Russia the summer of 1917 was a time of complete turmoil. The vast majority of the people were sick of the war. Soldiers deserted by the thousands; they voted for peace with their feet, Lenin said. In the cities there was a shortage of food. In the country peasants murdered the rich landowners and took over the land, and there were no police to object. The Provisional Government broke into factions that argued with one another.

Gradually the Bolsheviks gained power. Under Lenin's leadership they promised the people everything: free land for the peasants, food for the cities, control of the factories by the workers, and an end to the war. More and more members of the various soviets began to join the Bolshevik party.

Although Lenin himself dominated the party, its

leadership was supposed to be located in a Central Committee of nine members, including both Lenin and Stalin. Stalin, however, still played very little part in originating the policies to be followed. His main job was to explain the decisions of the Central Committee to members of the various soviets, and to make sure orders were followed.

This was the first of several jobs Stalin would hold that seemed relatively unimportant at the time, but would serve as building blocks toward his future power. When party members from outlying districts came to the capital, it was usually Stalin they met. Lenin, Kamenev, and most of the other leaders were far too busy to consult with minor party officials. So it was Stalin they conferred with. When they went back home, it was Stalin they remembered.

More important, the job gave Stalin a chance to study these party members from all over the country. In the back of his mind he filed away the things he learned about them: what their weaknesses were, how they could be influenced, which could be depended on. And this was Stalin's true genius: He almost never made a mistake in his judgement of men.

By the late summer of 1917 the Bolsheviks, or Communists, as they were now often called, had gained control of most of the soviets in Petrograd, in Moscow, and among the railroad workers. In the country as a

Lenin proclaims the Soviet state. In this painting of later years, Stalin is seen directly behind Lenin.

whole they were still a tiny minority. However, the real seat of power was Petrograd, the nation's capital, and here the Communists were the one tightly knit, disciplined group in the midst of chaos. Recognizing this, Lenin called for an armed revolution to seize power.

On November 6, Lenin told his party's Central Committee:

> The situation is critical in the extreme. It is absolutely clear that to delay the insurrection now would be fatal . . .
> We must not wait! We may lose everything! . . .
> The government is wavering. It must be given the finishing blow at all costs. To delay action will be fatal.

Arms were passed to workers and to soldiers who had joined the Communists. Quietly they moved into strategic positions throughout the city. And next morning signs appeared on the streets that read:

> From the Revolutionary Military Committee of the Petrograd Soviet of the Workers and Soldiers Deputies
>
> To the Citizens of Russia
>
> The Provisional Government has been overthrown. Governing power has passed into the hands of the agent of the Petrograd Soviet . . . the Revolutionary Military Committee.

Throughout the city the armed Communists moved in on what few bodies of the Provisional Government were still functioning. In some places there was brief fighting, but on the whole the agents of the Provisional Government, helpless and uncertain, simply gave up and walked out. Within a few hours Lenin's Bolsheviks were in control of the Russsian capital and of whatever government existed.*

What of Stalin in all this? Certainly he was there, following Lenin's orders. But his work was in the background. It is almost impossible to put a finger on any action in which he played a role. John Reed, an American who was in Petrograd at the time, wrote a book called *Ten Days That Shook the World*. In it he described in detail how the Communists seized power. Stalin's name appears twice in the entire book: once in a list of officials in the new government, and once as signed alongside Lenin's name, on a government order.

Stalin's days of real power still lay in the future.

---

* In many histories the capture of Petrograd by the Communists is known as the October Revolution, although it took place in November of the modern calendar. This is because the old calendar used under the tsar differed by about thirteen days from the calendar now used in Russia and in most of the world. By this old calendar the revolution did take place in October. In this book all dates follow the modern calendar.

4. Civil War

In their October Revolution the Communists gained control of Petrograd, but they did not control the rest of Russia. Almost every province, city, and town had its own government or none at all. Now the first job facing Lenin and his party was to gain control of the country as a whole, or as much of it as possible.

It was a formidable job. The war with Germany was still going on, and Lenin felt that his country must have peace at any price. Many of the other Bolshevik leaders, however, were opposed to this. They had always hoped that the Russian Revolution would lead the way to a revolution in Germany and other Western countries. They wanted to make peace, but only with a Germany controlled by Communists. To make peace while Germany was still under the control of capitalists, they argued, would be a betrayal of all German Communists.

Lenin argued that peace, now, was absolutely necessary so that the party could devote all its energy to what was happening in Russia.

In the argument that followed, Stalin sided with Lenin. Unlike many of the Communist leaders, he knew very little about the world outside Russia and did not worry much about it. His thoughts centered on what he understood close to him.

Gradually Lenin won the argument. He made peace with Germany, even though it meant the surrender of considerable territory.

But peace with Germany did not mean peace within Russia. Some of the soldiers who had been fighting the Germans now came over to the Communists; others followed officers who wanted to establish governments and armies in opposition.

What followed was one of the most terrible civil wars in history. Because red has always been considered the color of revolution, the Bolshevik armies were called Reds, the anti-Bolshevik forces Whites. The Reds were concentrated around Moscow and Petrograd, the two main cities. The White forces were scattered all over the country. Many of the White leaders were as opposed to one another as they were to the Reds. The result was like a storm at sea, like the passage of a hurricane, where the waves are lashed by winds first from one direction, then from another. Battles broke out within cities, and died out, and began again somewhere else. Britain, France, and the United States, all opposed to communism, furnished aid to the White forces wherever possible.

It was during this period that Joseph Stalin began to

gain the power that would eventually make him absolute dictator of all Russia and one of the most powerful men the world has ever known.

Under the new Communist government, Stalin's official title was commissar of nationalities, which meant he was to work with the minority groups, such as the Georgians and Ukrainians, whose lands made up a large part of the old Russian empire. These republics, as they were now called, were bound together in a federation, governed by the All-Russian Congress of Soviets. In the past, Stalin had always argued that, under communism, these groups would have the right of self-determination —they could choose for themselves whether to be independent or part of Russia. Now, somewhat to his and the party's surprise, many of these areas wanted to be not only independent, but non-Communist.

This was not what Stalin wanted. Speaking before the Congress of Soviets he demanded a change in policy. Self-determination, he said, should not mean the right of self-determination "for the bourgeoisie." It should apply only to "the toiling masses." Also it should "be used as a means in the struggle for socialism and . . . subordinated to the principles of socialism."

In other words, people should have the right of self-determination only as long as they determined to live under Bolshevik control.

At this time, however, with the country involved in

a desperate civil war, there was not much Stalin or the party could do about the matter. The first thing was to win the war.

When food supplies ran short in Moscow and Petrograd, Lenin sent Stalin to the city of Tsaritsyn in southern Russia where grain was plentiful. His job was to make sure this grain was collected and shipped north.

It was not a military job, but Lenin's order did give Stalin extraordinary powers to get and move the grain in any way possible. Before much grain had been collected, however, White troops attacked Tsaritsyn. Stalin suddenly found himself plunged into the middle of the fighting. He had no military training; nor had he ever been in a position of great power. But there was a ruthlessness in his character that, along with tremendous energy and ambition, made him hunger for military power. Now regarded as the highest ranking Communist in the area and armed with Lenin's order, he immediately took command of the fighting.

There were many people in Tsaritsyn who were anti-Communist, and Stalin began his fight by ordering the Cheka, the Communist secret police, to hunt down all these people. The Cheka headquarters were set up on a black barge in the Volga River. Here at night anyone suspected of treason to the Communist cause was brought, given a short trial, shot, and thrown overboard. Soon the entire city was in the grip of terror.

Stalin as he appeared
in the battle dress of a
Red army soldier in the
Civil War

The deliberate use of terror as a military weapon had
not been invented by Stalin. Trapped in a life-and-
death struggle, Lenin and the official Communist doctrine sponsored it. "How can you make a revolution
without shooting?" Lenin asked. And Felix Dzerzhinsky,
the head of the Cheka, had stated flatly, "We stand for
organized terror. . . . Terror is an absolute necessity during times of revolution."

Nobody understood this better than Stalin. By the
use of terror and by ruthlessly driving his men, he

stopped the enemy advance on Tsaritsyn. He collected quantities of grain and got it back to Moscow and Petrograd. He could not, however, actually defeat the White army in the area.

Leon Trotsky, the commissar for war, was officially in command of all Communist military forces. Trotsky was a man of extraordinary brilliance, a genius in half a dozen fields, and extremely conceited. He considered Stalin to be an uncouth boor. Stalin in turn loathed

Leon Trotsky, commissar for war, inspecting troops in Red Square, Moscow in the early 1920s

Trotsky with a deep personal hatred. Now he tried to blame all the trouble at Tsaritsyn on Trotsky and on the officers Trotsky had appointed. He telegraphed Lenin:

> If our military "specialists" (the shoe-makers!) had not been sleeping and wasting time, the line would not have been broken, and if the line is restored it will not be thanks to the military but in spite of them.

At the same time Stalin did not forget to glorify his own work:

> I am hurrying to the front. I am writing only on business. . . . Everything will be done to forestall possible surprises. You may rest assured that our hand will not flinch.

Lenin, who was an excellent judge of men, recognized the ability of both Stalin and Trotsky. He wanted to use both men to the best advantage and tried patiently to make them work together. But when Stalin began to write: "To be ignored" across Trotsky's orders, it was too much. Stalin was called back to Moscow, which was now the Communist capital.

It was a temporary defeat for Stalin, and one he never forgot or forgave. His hatred for Trotsky deepened.

Years later Trotsky himself would write:

> Thereafter, whenever I had occasion to tread on the corns of personal predilections, friendships, or vanities, Stalin carefully gathered up those people whose corns had been stepped on. . . . The leading spirits of Tsaritsyn became from that time on his principal tools.

Not long after Stalin's return to Moscow, the city of Perm, some 700 miles to the northeast, was captured by White forces. For a while it looked as if the White army might sweep west to capture Petrograd. Lenin sent a wire to Trotsky who was with the army in the south:

> There are several Party reports from around Perm about the catastrophic condition of the army and about drunkenness. . . . I thought of sending Stalin. I am afraid Smilga will be too soft. . . . Telegraph your opinion.

By this time Trotsky no longer looked on Stalin as a

simple boor to be ignored. He knew the man hated him and would do anything possible to get revenge for having been recalled from Tsaritsyn. But Trotsky knew also that when it came to cleaning up a mess, there was no man in Russia more effective than Joseph Stalin. Immediately he wired Lenin:

> I completely share your misgivings concerning the excessive softness of the Comrade who has gone there. I agree to Stalin's journey with powers from both the Party and the Revolutionary Council of War of the Republic for restoring order, purging the staff of commissars and severely punishing the guilty ...

In the Red army there were not only military officers, but each unit had a Bolshevik political officer called a commissar who sometimes had more to say about matters than the military. When Stalin joined what was left of the Bolshevik Third Army west of Perm, he immediately began cleaning out the commissars. Any he suspected of weakness he had shot. And he carefully replaced them with men of his own choosing, men he believed would be faithful to him when he needed them. Meanwhile he kept a stream of letters and telegrams flowing back to Lenin. In all of them he praised his own work and took careful shots at Trotsky without ever actually calling him by name:

> The units sent by the Commander in Chief
> are unreliable, partly even hostile to us,
> and are in need of serious filtering.

The failure of the army before he took over, Stalin wrote, was due to the fatigue and exhaustion of the army, to mismanagement of the army commander, and to criminal methods of administering the front by the Revolutionary Council of War.

Since Trotsky was the chairman of the Council of War, this amounted to a charge not only of failure, but almost of treason. Lenin, who now understood the personal feud between the two men, must have sighed as he read it.

Joseph Stalin was thirty-nine years old now, but with his dark, curly hair and big, drooping moustache, he looked younger. On March 24, 1919 he married for the second time. His bride's name was Nadezhda Alliluieva, a very pretty girl with dark hair and white skin. She was only sixteen, less than half of Stalin's age. Her father and Stalin had worked together in the Bolshevik party long before the revolution, and Stalin had known her since she was a baby.

There was, however, little time for romance. Within

a few weeks he was gone, this time to Petrograd, which was under attack by a White army from the west. Some of the Red troops defending the city had deserted and joined the enemy. It looked as if Petrograd itself would fall within a few days. Trotsky was deeply engaged on another front, and Stalin had asked to be sent to Petrograd to reorganize the defense. Lenin had agreed.

Stalin's work in Petrograd followed the pattern set in Tsaritsyn and Perm. He set the secret police to work hunting for traitors in the Red army and among the political commissars. Anyone suspected was removed from office and usually shot. The replacements, as before, were men selected by Stalin for their loyalty to him.

This version of the fighting at Tsaritsyn, painted many years later, shows Stalin directing the battle.

Next he turned his attention to the two forts that had gone over to the enemy. The most important of these was called Krasnaya Gorka.

The professional military men in Petrograd told Stalin it would be difficult and dangerous to attack Krasnaya Gorka from the sea. But since they controlled the land approaches, it would be fairly easy to capture the fort from land. It may have been this advice that made Stalin determined to use some naval forces; he wanted military glory for himself, and he also wanted to blacken the name of Trotsky's military specialists. He was, however, cautious and thorough as always. The attack he launched included ships and landing forces brought by sea. At the same time there was an attack by land and air.

The fort was captured without difficulty. Immediately Stalin wired Lenin:

> The naval specialists assert that the capture of Krasnaya Gorka from the sea runs counter to naval science. I only deplore this so-called science. The swift capture of Gorka came about as the result of the rudest intervention by me and other civilians in operational matters, even to the point of countermanding orders on land and sea and imposing our own.

I consider it my duty to announce that I shall continue to act in this way in the future in spite of all my reverence for science.

Years later much Russian history would be rewritten to make it seem as if Joseph Stalin had practically won the Civil War single-handed. An official government biography of Stalin stated:

It was Stalin who directly inspired and organized the major victories of the Red Army. Wherever the destinies of the revolution were being decided in battle, there the Party sent Stalin. It was he who drew up the chief strategic plans and who directed the decisive military operations. At Tsaritsyn, Perm, at Petrograd . . . everywhere Stalin's iron will and strategic genius caused victory for the revolution. . . . With Stalin's name are linked the most glorious victories of the Red Army.

This book was supposed to have been written by official Russian historians. Very few persons knew that it was Stalin himself who had written most of it.

Actually the Communist victory was largely due to

Trotsky's military brilliance. Stalin's role was that of a ruthless, but effective, troubleshooter—a man who could weed out and destroy those who were opposed to communism behind the lines and who, by the use of terror, could force others to cooperate.

Toward the end of the Civil War, Kamenev made a motion in the Bolshevik Central Committee that Stalin be awarded the medal of the Order of the Red Banner. Most of the other members looked at him in amazement. "The Red Banner," one said, "is for truly heroic work in the war. Would you tell me what Comrade Stalin has done to win it?"

Bukharin, who was a friend of Kamenev's, laughed. "You know Stalin," he said. "He can't live unless he has what someone else has."

So Stalin was awarded the Order of the Red Banner through the help of Kamenev and Bukharin. No mention, however, was made of this in later years when both men were executed at Stalin's command.

5. Lenin's Death

By the end of 1920 the various White armies were largely defeated, and the Communists were in full control of the government. But Russia itself lay in almost total ruin. Some two million men had been killed in combat, either in World War I or in the Civil War that followed. Seven million men, women, and children had died of starvation or disease. About two million had fled the country to escape the rule of the Bolsheviks.

In reaching for power Lenin had promised the people just about everything they could ask for. There would be free land for the peasants, he promised. The workers would own the factories in which they worked. There would be freedom of the press, of speech, and of political parties.

Once the Bolsheviks were in power, however, things changed swiftly. Lenin had hoped the Russian Revolution would be followed by Communist revolutions in many other countries. This did not happen, and now the Bolsheviks found themselves surrounded by capitalist nations that would have liked to see a counterrevolution

This photograph of Lenin and Stalin was taken at Lenin's home in Gorki in 1922.

overthrow the Russian Communists. In order to maintain their own dictatorship, the Communists quickly abolished all other political parties. Freedom of speech and freedom of the press were outlawed. The land, the factories, and practically every business in Russia were taken over by the government—and the government was the Communist party.

The Communists' main strength lay in the cities, and getting food to the people of the cities soon became their most urgent and desperate problem. To do this the government ruled that the peasants could not sell their crops or animals on an open market. Instead, these were confiscated by the government at low, government-fixed prices. Often the peasants were left without enough food for themselves. The peasants, in turn, hid their supplies or refused to grow those crops on which the government had fixed low prices.

By 1921 famine stalked the country. But there was not only a shortage of food, there was also a shortage of clothing, houses, fuel, transportation. Thousands of mismanaged factories closed because of a lack of supplies. Even the people who had helped the Bolsheviks gain power were now turning against them.

Lenin, who was always willing to admit his own errors when he recognized them, said publicly, "We were wrong." He began to abolish many laws passed during the Civil War, and instituted what he called the

New Economic Policy. This was a partial return to capitalism. The peasants were allowed to sell some part of their produce for the best prices they could get. In the cities individual merchants could operate some types of shops. Gradually the country began to return to normal.

In these great decisions on policy, Joseph Stalin played little part. His name was still unknown to most of the Russian people. But within the Communist party he was, little by little, acquiring more power than even Lenin realized.

During the Civil War and in the chaotic days of starvation that followed it, Lenin and Trotsky and most of the party leaders had been too busy with other things to worry about building a personal political machine. Not Joseph Stalin. A man of tremendous energy, he seemed to have more hours in his day than other people. Frequently he worked until four or five in the morning. He was always willing to take on a new job —so long as it enhanced his power. By the end of the Civil War he was the commissar for nationalities and a member of the Military Revolutionary Council and the Political Bureau. The Politburo, as it was usually called, was the small group of men, including Lenin, who dominated the Communist party.

What would prove more important in the long run, Stalin was also a member of the Organization Bureau (the Orgburo) and of the Commissariat of the Workers' and Peasants' Inspectorate. These were jobs that other party leaders paid little attention to. But they gave Stalin a chance to travel about the country and to meet party members and the leaders of small soviets in distant towns and cities. More important, he had the power to remove some leaders and to replace them with others.

Stalin worked slowly. He seemed never to hurry. He had incredible patience. He would stand for long minutes on a stairway, or on the sidewalk, puffing his pipe and listening to the complaints of the minor officials he visited. And he listened more carefully than anyone knew. If he found an official who admired Lenin or Trotsky too much, Stalin would find a reason to remove him from office and put someone else in his place.

To the men who lost their jobs, this could be a very serious matter. While many people were starving, Communist officials got extra rations. Even after the period of starvation had passed, the Communist party controlled practically all jobs. Stalin wanted men who would follow Communist discipline without question, and he had a true genius for picking such men. Some of those he selected were criminals, men he had known from his own days in prison. Gradually he built his political machine throughout the cities and towns of Russia.

On April 2, 1922, at Lenin's suggestion, Stalin was made general secretary of the Central Committee of the Communist party. Again it was a job that did not seem very important; the truly imporant party leaders like Lenin, Kamenev, Zinoviev, and Bukharin did not want it. But this job, like the ones with the Orgburo and the Inspectorate, gave Stalin power to remove or promote officials—important ones now. It was a job he would hold for thirty years, and it was the one that would eventually make him dictator.

Less than two months after Stalin became general secretary, a blood vessel burst in Lenin's brain. The man who had dominated the Communist party and all Russia lay half paralyzed and barely able to speak.

In the Kremlin—the complex of government buildings surrounded by a wall where most party leaders lived and worked—there began an immediate struggle to take over Lenin's power. It was a quiet struggle; the people of Russia heard nothing and knew nothing about it. But for the men involved, and for millions of others who did not even know the struggle was going on, it literally would mean life or death.

At this time the four best known Communists, in addition to Lenin, were Trotsky, Kamenev, Zinoviev, and Bukharin. Of these Trotsky was by far the most popular. He had created the Red army, and the army adored him. It is quite possible that by using the army, once Lenin was out of the way, Trotsky could have made himself military dictator. But in all the struggle that followed he never once tried this.

Kamenev was president of the Moscow Soviet; Zinoviev headed the soviet in Petrograd. These were the two largest cities in Russia, and the Communist party was tightly organized in both, giving each man great power. Through his various jobs Stalin controlled most of the soviets in the outlying districts.

Kamenev used his power lightly. He was not a particularly ambitious man and was conscious of his own shortcomings. Zinoviev had an entirely different personality. A short, dark man, he was driven by ambitions that outran his talent. Although he could be charming at times, nobody really trusted him, and with reason.

It was probably Zinoviev who approached Kamenev and Stalin with the proposition that they work together against Trotsky. Although Trotsky was popular with the general public, his arrogance and generally overbearing attitude made him highly unpopular with other party officials. Stalin was quite ready to join with Kamenev and Zinoviev. But these two had no idea what they were letting themselves in for. They still thought of Stalin as a man good at getting some particular job done, but not fitted for real leadership.

This struggle for leadership—and it would prove to be a deadly struggle before it was over—was not based on personalities alone. Important matters of Communist policy were involved, and perhaps the most important of all concerned discipline within the party itself. Both

Stalin and Trotsky believed in a Communist government built on the teachings of Marx and Lenin. They differed on how such a government should maintain itself once in power. How much power should be centered in the hands of a small group of leaders? How much freedom of speech was to be allowed the other party members? Should they be free to criticize the party leadership on some things, or be expected to obey all orders blindly? And how much force should be used in carrying out these orders?

Trotsky believed in both discipline and force. At the same time he believed that with good leadership, it should be possible to find a balance between force and freedom. In some ways Trotsky was an idealist. He believed that once the principles of socialism were made clear to the masses of the people, they would understand, accept these principles, and follow the Communist party willingly.

Stalin had no more faith in the masses than he had had in the government of the tsars. He believed that any government must depend on force to maintain itself, and he believed the power to use this force should be concentrated in very few hands. And Stalin understood better than anyone else the power that his various jobs had concentrated in his own hands.

While Lenin lay ill, news of the government was still brought to him, and he too began to realize how much power Stalin had acquired. Also he had serious doubts about how Stalin would use that power if it ever became absolute. Half paralyzed, able to work only a few minutes each day, Lenin began to prepare what he called a "bombshell." This was a paper, later called Lenin's Testament, which pointed out how pitiless Stalin had been in the past and asked that he be removed from his position of general secretary.

It was a very dangerous time in Stalin's life. If Lenin recovered from his illness, if he were able to deliver his "bombshell" before the Party Congress, it was almost certain Stalin would be removed, one way or another.

Stalin knew this. By now he had his own spies working in Lenin's home. In fact, Stalin's young wife worked for a while as one of Lenin's secretaries and reported to her husband what Lenin was trying to do.

Lenin's illness continued for almost two years. Several times it seemed that he was about to recover, that soon he would be able to face the Communist Party Congress and make his attack upon Stalin. But in December 1922 he had a second stroke.

At the congress in December which Lenin had hoped to attend, Stalin's proposal to establish a new and more powerful federation of the Soviet states was accepted. It would be called the Union of Soviet Socialist Republics, or the U.S.S.R. Lenin himself lay helpless and unable to participate in the work of the congress.

Still, he refused to give up. He fought his illness as furiously as he had fought capitalism all his life. In March 1923 he had a third stroke, but by early January of 1924, it once more looked as if he would recover.

Then on January 21, 1924, Lenin died. In all probability his death was the result of his long illness. Several years later, however, Leon Trotsky would ask in a biography of Stalin: "What was Stalin's actual role at the time of Lenin's illness? Did not the disciple do something to expedite his master's death?"

Trotsky's answer was to imply, though he could not prove it, that Stalin had in some way poisoned Lenin. Even today there is no proof, one way or the other.

6. The Struggle for Power

According to the theories taught by Marx, Engels, and
Lenin, a true Communist government must begin with
what they called a "dictatorship of the proletariat." By
this they meant that a Communist government must, in
its early stages, be under the absolute control of the
working class of people—people who, in Russia at least,
had largely been without money or property under
capitalism. But as time went on, they said, conditions
under communism would improve so much that everybody would have everything they needed, and there
would be no need for government. At this point government would "wither away."

That was the ideal, but Joseph Stalin knew perfectly
well that very few men, given great power, would ever
release that power willingly. A government might be
destroyed, but it would never wither away. In Russia
the "dictatorship of the proletariat" had become the
dictatorship of one political party. Until his death, Lenin
had dominated that party. Now Stalin was determined to
take over. To do this he would need to surpass, possibly

to destroy, Leon Trotsky, Kamenev, Zinoviev, and many other Communists who were better known than he was.

As usual, Stalin worked slowly, carefully, and in such a devious manner that the other Communist leaders did not understand what he was up to. It was one of the strangest and most effective campaigns of his career. In it he turned Lenin, who had been an atheist, into a kind of Communist "god" and then made himself, Joseph Djugashvili, the chief apostle and high priest of the new religion.

Ever since the days of Karl Marx, communism had been a strange, almost mystical blend of atheism and religion. Marx himself had written that formal religion "is the opiate of the people," and in Russia the Communist party had made every effort to abolish all religion. Churches had been closed and priests sent into exile. In the schools children were taught that religion was simply a set of lies used by rich persons to keep the poor from rebellion.

Yet at the same time many of the Old Bolsheviks had believed in and worshiped the Communist party almost as if it were itself a religion. They had no faith in democracy. For one thing, most of them knew little about it. Also, their own propaganda over the years had convinced them that democracy could not work. Instead they believed that the only hope for the future of Russia —the future of the whole world—lay in communism.

They believed devoutly that, although the individual party member might be wrong, the party itself was always right.

Now Stalin set out to expand this mystical belief in the party to include Lenin as the party god and Joseph Djugashvili as Lenin's disciple. He began his campaign with a funeral oration for Lenin, a strange speech that

Immense crowds press close to Lenin's coffin as his funeral procession slowly moves past the walls of the Kremlin in Red Square, Moscow.

sounded almost as if he were back in the seminary chanting a liturgy. Standing beside Lenin's casket he cried:

> In departing from us Comrade Lenin enjoined on us to hold high and keep pure the great calling of member of the party.
>
> We vow to thee, Comrade Lenin, that we will with honor fulfill this thy commandment.
>
> In departing from us Comrade Lenin enjoined on us to guard the unity of our party as the apple of our eye.
>
> We vow to thee, Comrade Lenin, that we will with honor fulfill this thy commandment.
>
> In departing from us Comrade Lenin enjoined on us to guard and strengthen the dictatorship of the proletariat.
>
> We vow to thee, Comrade Lenin, that we will with honor fulfill this thy commandment.

And on and on . . .

In Russia the Communist party controlled every single newspaper and magazine, and through his job as general secretary of the party, Stalin had carefully placed his own men in charge of them. Now the papers and magazines began to print stories about Lenin that made him appear to have been a superman who never made an error. Religious-looking pictures and statues of Lenin began to appear throughout the country. The name of Petrograd, the city where communism had first gained power, was changed to Leningrad.

These were the first steps in Stalin's campaign to win the battle for power and to oust the other party leaders. His first target was Trotsky. Stalin, working closely at first with Kamenev and Zinoviev, knew that Trotsky was still too powerful to be attacked directly. But in the past Trotsky had often disagreed with Lenin, and now the papers began to mention this. If Lenin had always been right, then naturally anyone who disagreed with him had been wrong. The more Lenin was built up, the more Trotsky was torn down.

It took time, but Stalin always had time. He had infinite patience. Little by little he destroyed Trotsky's popularity with the people. Little by little he built himself up as Lenin's devoted disciple. And at the same time, acting as general secretary of the Communist party, he kept moving men who were loyal to him into strategic positions.

Eventually the struggle between Trotsky and the triumvirs—as Kamenev, Zinoviev, and Stalin came to be

Five days after Lenin's death, Stalin addressed the party congress at a memorial meeting in Lenin's honor.

called—moved into the open. Although the fight was caused mainly by the personal ambitions of the men involved, there were also important political issues. Trotsky pointed out that it had always been a basic belief of communism that a true Socialist revolution could not be successful in one country alone; he then accused the triumvirs of not working to spread revolution from Russia to the rest of Europe. Stalin replied that he too wanted world revolution, but the important thing at this time was to build a secure base in Russia. When Trotsky claimed that the triumvirs were destroying free speech and self-criticism within the party, the triumvirs replied that Lenin himself had demanded party unity. Now, they said, Trotsky was working against the orders of Lenin. Trotsky in turn wrote a book that told of the many times Kamenev and Zinoviev had disagreed with Lenin.

Throughout the struggle Stalin had one tremendous advantage: neither Trotsky, Kamenev nor Zinoviev had any suspicion of Stalin's own overwhelming ambition. Most of the time he managed to remain in the background just as he had done during the strikes and demonstrations many years before. Kamenev and Zinoviev led the attack on Trotsky. Stalin backed them, yet always managed to give the impression of personal goodwill. At one meeting of the Politburo, Zinoviev refused to speak to Trotsky. Kamenev barely nodded to him. But Stalin happily shook hands with everybody. For a long while he managed to maintain a position from which he could have switched to Trotsky's side had Trotsky appeared the victor.

Since Trotsky still underrated Stalin, he centered his own attacks on Kamenev and Zinoviev. As a result Stalin was the only one of the four whose political image was not badly damaged by the fight. Trotsky was hurt worst of all. Bit by bit his popularity was diminished. Army officers who admired him and might have defended him were demoted or transferred to remote parts of the country. Finally in April 1925 Trotsky was forced to resign his office as commissar of war.

Almost immediately Stalin turned on the men who had helped him demote Trotsky. He joined with three other party leaders, Bukharin, Rykov, and Tomsky, and with their help began the same kind of campaign against Kamenev and Zinoviev which he had waged against Trotsky.

The biggest public issue involved was the continuation of Stalin's dispute with Trotsky over whether or not communism could be successful in Russia, even if no other countries staged revolutions. Kamenev and Zinoviev had been willing to gibe at Trotsky's theory of "permanent revolution" simply to discredit Trotsky. Both later admitted this. But basically they were in agreement with the Communist doctrine that socialism, to be successful, must spread from one country to another.

In opposition to this, Stalin put forward what was probably his most original idea. Russia, he said, could build a Socialist society all by itself. He had never known or been as interested in the outside world as many of the Old Bolsheviks. He had always kept his eyes on Russia. He did not yet argue against the Communist doctrine of world revolution. World revolution, he said, was always to be hoped for. But "socialism in one country," as the idea came to be called, was possible. Russia, Stalin said, could build such a society with no help from the rest of the world.

The idea proved quickly popular. The great mass of the Russian people, even the members of the Communist party, were weary of revolution. The country was still on the edge of famine, and the idea of "permanent revolution" frightened the people. "Socialism in one country" seemed to promise peace and security.

Another issue that divided Kamenev, Zinoviev, and their followers from Stalin's new allies was a matter of economics. Everyone agreed that Russia, or the Soviet Union as it was often called, desperately needed both new industry and greater food production. The question was how this could be achieved. Kamenev and Zinoviev wanted to persuade vast numbers of peasants to move from small, individual farms to big cooperatives using

In 1920 Old Bolsheviks Trotsky (far left), Kamenev (second from right), and Stalin (far right) saluted the crowds. By 1928 Trotsky and Kamenev had been deposed, and Stalin held the reins of power.

farm machinery furnished by the government. Bukharin, Rykov, and Tomsky favored letting the most prosperous farmers, called *kulaks*, increase the amount of land they were now farming.

In this argument Stalin took little part. He sided with his new allies, but stayed in the middle as much as possible.

Gradually Kamenev and Zinoviev, like Trotsky, were forced out of their important jobs. Stalin, as general secretary, quickly dismissed their followers, replacing them with men loyal to himself.

By now Stalin's new partners, Bukharin, Rykov, and Tomsky, were beginning to realize that they too had been trapped in a spider's web. Bukharin was a soft man who had always been more interested in the theory of communism as an ideal government than in the way things actually worked. Now he was seeing the truth, and it terrified him. He went to call on Kamenev.

"Stalin's going to kill us all," he said over and over. "He doesn't care what happens to the revolution. He doesn't care what happens to Russia. All he wants is power. He hates the peasants because he can't control them. You remember his theory of intense pleasure."

Kamenev nodded. He was thinking of a summer night several years before, when he and Stalin had still been allies. As they talked together over a bottle of wine, Stalin had said, "You know, the greatest pleasure in life is to choose your enemy, to plan your vengeance, carefully, over a long time, and then to put the knife in his back and go home to sleep."

The statement had made a deep impression on Kamenev, who had repeated it to several other Bolsheviks. Now he said, "I know his theory. But what can we do?"

To this Bukharin had no answer. He was like a man already doomed.

It is probable that Stalin, who by now had his secret police almost everywhere, soon learned of the meeting between Kamenev and Bukharin. If so, he did not hurry his plans. He knew that Trotsky, Bukharin, and the other Old Bolsheviks were still too popular to be murdered or even jailed without causing trouble. And Stalin had patience. He could plan his vengeance carefully, over a long time. He gave orders for Kamenev to be sent to Siberia. Meanwhile Bukharin and Rykov, along with other Old Bolsheviks, found their jobs and power slipping away.

By 1928 the Politburo and the Central Committee of the Communist party were packed with Stalin's hand-picked men—men who would take his orders with no questions asked. Stalin himself still held no official job more important than that of general secretary. But he had become the absolute dictator of all Russia.

7. Death and the Five-Year Plan

While Stalin, Trotsky, and the other Communist leaders waged their battle for personal power, the great mass of the Russian people had struggled merely to stay alive. The country over which Stalin finally gained control was in desperate condition. There was no longer the actual starvation which had followed the Civil War, but there was a very real threat that famine would once again become widespread.

At this time Russia had approximately 25 million peasant families living in rural areas or small villages. These farmers were officially divided into three groups. There was the poorest group made up of about 5 to 8 million families, most of them so backward that they still used wooden plows. There was a middle group of 15 to 18 million families, and then a group of 1½ or 2 million fairly well-to-do families, which were called *kulaks*. There were also some large, state-owned farms. The Communists had promoted these ever since gaining power in 1917, but only a relatively few peasants had been willing to join them.

Under the Communist law, the peasants were supposed to sell a certain part of their produce to the government at a fixed, low price. But the price of manufactured goods, which the peasants could buy in return, was high. There was, in fact, an acute shortage of manufactured goods at any price. As a result, the farmers held back their surplus produce whenever possible. In the cities the food shortage grew worse and worse. There was also a shortage of clothing and housing. Unemployment was widespread.

The difficulties of life in the cities posed a particular problem for the Communists. The main strength of the party had always been among the industrial workers, but now even they were complaining. Obviously something had to be done.

Early in 1928 Stalin made an inspection tour of some of the Russian farms. He dressed as usual in a semi-military uniform: a brown coat with a high collar and dark trousers stuffed into the tops of leather boots. He had a short stemmed pipe in his mouth. He listened patiently while the kulaks complained about the government-fixed price of grain and while minor Communist officials explained why they had been unable to collect as much foodstuff as the government expected. When they had finished, Stalin made a brief speech.

"You tell me," he said, "the quotas are too high and cannot be filled. Where does this idea come from? I have seen dozens of your prosecuting and judicial officials. Nearly all of them are living in the homes of kulaks; they board and lodge with them, and of course they are only too anxious to live in peace with them. Clearly nothing effective or useful to the Soviet state can be expected from these officials."

Stalin did not shout, and his expression was not threatening. "I propose," he said, "first, the immediate delivery of all grain surpluses from the kulaks at government prices. Second, kulaks refusing to obey the law [should] be prosecuted . . . and their grain surpluses [should] be confiscated."

That was all. Stalin smiled and went back to Moscow, and set in motion what would be called the First Five-Year Plan. For literally millions upon millions of Russians, it would prove to be a plan for death by starvation, torture, and overwork. Probably there has been nothing quite like it in all history.

The basic purpose of the Five-Year Plan was to change the U.S.S.R. from a backward agricultural nation into a great, modern, industrial power. To do this, Stalin divided the plan into two major parts: One was to deal with the development of new mines, factories, and power plants; the other with agriculture. Both parts of the plan were to be carried on at the same time as much as possible.

Since Russia at this point had relatively little industry, nearly all the material for the creation of new mines and factories must be bought from other countries. But because of this same lack of industry, Russia had no manufactured goods with which to pay for these purchases. Nor could she borrow money, because the capitalist countries refused to loan money to Communists.

The things Russia did have in plenty were natural resources, land, and people. Stalin planned to use people to produce farm crops on the land. Then these crops could be sold to other countries for the steel, concrete, and machines necessary to build industry.

There was, of course, one problem. Despite the vast amount of land and the number of peasant farmers, Russia was not producing enough food for its own people, let alone for sale abroad. Part of the Five-Year Plan was to increase the production of food.

To do this Stalin planned to force the peasants to live and work on large, collective farms. This would have two benefits: First, working together and using machinery supplied by the state, the peasants would produce more food than before. Second, it would be far easier for the government to collect the produce from a few large farms under central control than from a vast number of small ones with individual managers.

The trouble was that the peasants did not want to give up their farms and homes. Many simply refused to move to the collective farms, and the only way for the state to move them was by force.

Joseph Stalin was never afraid to use force. The government officials who in the past had not collected all the grain expected of them quickly disappeared, sent to slave labor camps or simply shot. In their place appeared an army of secret police. If a peasant refused to move to a collective farm, or tried to hide part of the produce from his own farm, the police moved in. They took everything they could find: horses, cows, pigs, sheep, corn, and wheat. Frequently they burned the peasant's home. Sometimes the police would raid an entire village of peasants. Then with the police wagons and trucks piled high with foodstuff and livestock, they would go, leaving the peasants to die of hunger.

The treatment of the kulaks, the well-to-do farmers, was even worse than that of the poor peasants. Stalin simply ordered the "elimination of the kulaks as a class." Their property was confiscated. Many were shot or starved; thousands were sent to slave labor camps to die of exposure and overwork.

In their own hopeless way both the kulaks and the poor peasants fought back. They planted only enough wheat and corn for their own use and hid this from the police. Rather than turning their livestock over to the police, they killed and ate it. Within a few years the number of horses in Russia dropped from 36 million to less than 16 million, the number of cattle from almost 67 million to less than 34 million.

Peasants threshing wheat on the "New Life" collective farm during the First Five-Year Plan

Stalin in turn ordered that anyone who killed a horse or cow, a sheep or pig without authority would himself be killed by the police.

There is no doubt that at this point the peasants would have staged a revolution and overthrown Stalin's government, had they been able. But Russia was a country of vast distances. Communications were poor, and the peasants had no way of getting together or even of knowing what was happening in other areas.

There had been hunger in Russia before the start of the Five-Year Plan. Soon there was actual starvation, often worst in the very sections where the most food was normally produced. Somewhere between 5 and 10 million peasants—there was no way to count—died during the early years of the Five-Year Plan. Some were shot by the police; some died in labor camps; most of them simply starved. Whole families died in their homes. Sometimes police, descending on a village to confiscate food, found the place empty except for gaunt and rotting corpses. In some places children, the last persons left alive, roamed the streets in packs like hungry dogs.

Even so, the peasants who survived were gradually forced into collective farms. From these the government could collect its quota of grain with minimum effort. And here men who had never before seen a tractor might eventually learn to use one.

For the other half of his program—the industrialization of the nation—Stalin and the Communist party used the people of the cities as harshly as they used the peasants. Often men and women were assigned to jobs by government order, with no right to choose where or at what they would work. They were forbidden to move from one town to another, or even to quit one job for a better one without government permission. Food, clothing, and housing were all strictly rationed, and nothing could be bought without a ration card. But if a worker, man or woman, missed a day on the job without some definite excuse, even if he were as little as twenty minutes late to work, he could be fired. If fired, he lost his place to live. He lost his ration card.

And the loss of a ration card was almost like a sentence of death.

Many of those who lost jobs were then sent to work at new industries being developed in the Siberian wilderness. Working in temperatures that were often far below zero, without enough food or shelter, they struggled to dig mines and canals. They cut down entire forests for lumber, some to be used in Russia, some to be sold abroad. Men who had never used a machine in their lives were set to work to build factories and cities where there had been nothing but barren wastes.

Because the farm products were not enough to pay for the machinery and tools that had to be purchased abroad, the Communist government sold the great art collections that had belonged to the tsars. By one method or another, the people were forced to give up their jewels, gold, family silver, and anything that could be turned into capital.

Every kind of business now was placed under the direct supervision of the Communist party. The party then assigned every factory a quota of goods that had to be produced, whether it was so many shoes, nuts, bolts, or tractors. A plant manager who failed to meet his quota might be demoted, sent to Siberia, or shot. As a result desperate measures were taken. Men and women were forced to work until they died of exhaustion. A shoe factory that did not get enough leather to produce its quota of shoes might make shoes of something else, even if they fell apart the first time they were worn.

No one dared complain because it was the party that made all the plans, and according to Communist theory, the party could never be wrong. Therefore it had to be the men who carried out the orders who were wrong. If a factory did not meet its quota of shoes, the district manager would say the factory manager had done this deliberately because he was trying to sabotage the Communist party. The factory manager would blame the shop manager. The shop manager would blame the workers. Men would simply disappear, shot by firing squads or sent to slave labor camps.

There were two things that held the country together at this time. First, there was the iron discipline of the Communist party and the deliberate use of terror. Sitting in his Kremlin office Stalin told a foreign newspaper reporter, "We learned by experience that the only way to deal with our enemies was to inflict upon them the most merciless policies of suppression." By enemies he meant any Russians unwilling to accept the Communist dictatorship. And he added, "We Bolsheviks do not confine ourselves to using weapons of terror, but go further—our aim is to liquidate completely the whole class of property owners." "Liquidate" was the Communist word for murder.

There was, however, a second and far better thing that helped to unite the country. Despite the incredible waste and confusion, new mines were dug in the wilderness; new factories, power plants, and entire cities were built. In an amazingly short time Russia did change from a backward, almost entirely agricultural country into a modern, industrial power.

If the Russian people had ever known democracy and personal liberty, this progress would not have been

Dedication of the Dnieprostroy Dam, one of Russia's huge hydroelectric projects of the early 1930s

enough to justify the savage methods of Stalin and the Communist party. The Russians, however, had lived for centuries under the dictatorship of the tsars. For many the dictatorship of the Communists was no worse than what they had known before. More important, there was now for the first time a dream of a better future. Communism, they were told, would eventually abolish all classes, make all men equal, with justice and better living conditions for all. Actually it merely replaced one group of rulers with another. But most of the new rulers came from the poor, and to many of these people communism offered the first real chance to improve their lives. For the first time in Russia a free education was offered to almost everyone. Poor factory workers and peasants now had a chance, through education, to move on to better jobs. Many Communists truly believed that, in the long run, what they were doing would benefit all mankind.

8. "The Great Stalin"

On December 21, 1929 Stalin was fifty years old, and the Communist party ordered the Russian people to celebrate. Probably Stalin himself did not give the order. This was done by officials who wanted to flatter him. But as Stalin bossed the Communist party, it is certain he agreed with the plans.

It was a strange and remarkable affair.

Almost exactly ten years before this, Lenin, the true founder of Russian communism, had celebrated his fiftieth birthday. Lenin had been a ruthless man, capable of any type of cruelty to achieve his ends, but he had truly believed in the benefits of socialism and had been deeply loved by many of the people around him. A genius whose brilliance was admitted even by his enemies, he had never felt any need to glorify himself, and his fiftieth birthday had been a quiet affair attended by a handful of Communist leaders. It was only after Lenin's death that he was elevated to the role of party god on Stalin's orders.

Stalin himself ruled by terror. Perhaps this is why

he needed a different kind of celebration. Also he was ready now to move up and take his place alongside Marx and Lenin as a god of communism.

On Stalin's birthday every newspaper, every magazine, every publication in Russia printed huge pictures of him. They published story after story that praised him so wildly that they would have been laughed at anywhere else. No one in the Soviet Union dared laugh.

He was no longer called just Joseph Stalin. He was Great Stalin, the Founder of Communism, the Father of Peoples, and the Hope of the World's Poor. He was the man who had created and led the Red army. (There was no longer any mention of Trotsky except to say that he had been an enemy of the people who had tried to destroy the work of Stalin.)

A Russian general wrote an article saying that during the Civil War, Stalin had always known what the enemy was planning and had been right on every decision. Another article claimed that Lenin had relied on Stalin to do all the important work. Indeed, Lenin began to be pushed gently into the background. It was Great Stalin, the All-Wise, who had really done everything.

Stalin's birthday celebration was not a one-day affair. It went on for weeks. In fact it would continue until Stalin's death twenty-three years later. Cities changed their names to honor him. There was a Stalingrad, a

Stalino, a Stalinabad, Stalinsk, Stalinogorsk. Mountains and canals, factories and schools were named for him.

Public meetings did not begin with prayer or the playing of the national anthem; they began with praise of Great Stalin and ended with praise of the Father of Peoples. But this was not all. Stalin read few books and knew nothing about art, but he had always been jealous of some of the Old Bolsheviks who were broadly educated and cultured men. So now one writer claimed that Stalin "has always been distinguished by his profound understanding of literature." Another said, "In reality certain pronouncements of Aristotle have only been fully deciphered and expressed by Stalin." And another declared that "Socrates and Stalin are the highest peaks of human intelligence."

And still this was not all. There was another and even stranger phase of the birthday celebration.

Stalin's fiftieth birthday came just as the First Five-Year Plan moved toward its peak. All across Russia literally millions of people were starving. More millions suffered in the slave labor camps of Siberia. But from the hungry, the overworked, and the dying came letters and telegrams signed by hundreds of thousands of persons praising Stalin. Newspapers reprinted the letters, carrying solid page after page of the signed names.

Many signatures, of course, had been forced, signed in terror. But many of the persons toiling in the labor

In this painting Stalin speaks at a Communist Party Congress soon after his fiftieth birthday. He stands symbolically in front of a bust of Lenin.

camps simply did not believe Stalin was to blame. Stalin was the head of the party, and the party was always right. Everything they read, everything they were taught, confirmed this belief. If things went wrong, if people suffered and died, it was the fault of the unknown, mysterious people who hated the party and tried to destroy its work.

The adulation, the fulsome praise heaped on Stalin, was enough to turn the stomach of a goat. Stalin himself knew perfectly well that much of it came from men who hated him, but who hoped to get ahead by flattery. It amused him to see them grovel. But at the same time he put on an act of mock humility. In a message to the Russian people, he thanked them for his birthday celebration by saying: "Your congratulations and greetings I place to the credit of the great party of the working class which bore me and raised me in its own image and likeness."

It was a shrewd statement. It sounded modest. But in the Soviet Union the Communist party was not only all-powerful, it was supposed to be perfect, incapable of error; therefore a man "raised in its own image and likeness" must also be perfect.

To foreign newspapermen who came to interview him, Stalin put on an act of being not only modest but pleasant, gracious, almost shy. Some of these reporters knew about the slave labor camps, the burned villages, and the piled corpses of peasants. They knew that with a single word Stalin could have stopped these things. And yet they found this difficult to believe when they talked with him. There seemed to be no possible connection between the man sitting behind his desk, smiling easily, and the horrible orders that came out of this same office.

When a German newspaperman asked Stalin about the extravagant flattery being heaped on him, Stalin shook his head, looking faintly worried. "It is wrong," he said. "I would stop it if I could. Because I am only a pupil of Lenin, and my only desire is to be worthy of him."

When an American reporter asked how it felt to be a dictator, Stalin said, "I am no dictator. . . . Under the Communist system no one man or group of men can dictate. Decisions are made by the party."

Certainly Stalin knew—and he knew that the reporter knew—that he was a dictator.

Neither flattery nor power, however, made any immediate change in Stalin's daily life. He had never had money and did not care about it. Now, though the government paid him, he tossed the money into a desk drawer and forgot about it. In fact, he had no need for money. Whatever he wanted he ordered, and it was brought to him.

His physical wants were simple. He could have had one of the tsar's palaces, or all of them, but he and his family continued to live in a tiny apartment in one of the Kremlin buildings. He had three children now. There was a boy, Vasily, born in 1919, and a little girl Svetlana. Jacob, his son by his first wife, had also come to live with them. The little girl was Stalin's favorite, but actually she got to see very little of her father. He liked to work late at night and so slept late in the morning. Shortly before noon he would eat his breakfast, sometimes with Svetlana on his lap. Then he walked to his office in a nearby building. Here he stayed at his work until three or four the next morning.

It was a huge office, fifty feet long by twenty feet wide. The carpet and walls were dark green. The only furniture was Stalin's desk and a long table with chairs around it. On the wall directly above the table hung two large photographs, one of Karl Marx and one of Lenin. There were no books, no flowers, no plants, not even maps or newspapers. If Stalin wanted anything, he rang a bell; a secretary appeared like a genie and brought what was asked for.

Besides the secretary's bell, there was a battery of telephones, and it was with these Stalin did most of his work. Direct lines led to the offices of government officials all over the country. Since Stalin liked to work at night, and since it never occurred to him to be considerate of other persons, he was quite likely to make his telephone calls at one, two, or three o'clock in the morning. If he got no answer, or if he learned that some official had gone home to bed, it might well mean the end of the man's job.

There was another line on Stalin's desk that led directly to the basement of Lubyanka prison. It was here that political prisoners were most often tortured or killed. And now that power was in his hands, Stalin was about to begin a reign of terror more senseless and incredible than anything that had gone before it.

9. The Growth of Fear

Joseph Stalin was no coward. He did not fear pain. Perhaps he did not even fear death. What he did fear was the loss of power, because power was the one thing for which he had an ever-increasing hunger.

Since he himself had been willing to trick and destroy anyone who stood in his way, it was impossible for him now to trust anyone else. Suspicion ate at him constantly, and as his power grew, so grew his fear and suspicion of the men closest to him.

There was, in fact, some reason for Stalin's fear. Although Trotsky had been expelled from Russia he wrote articles and books abroad, attacking Stalin. These were officially barred from publication in the U.S.S.R., but copies were often smuggled in to circulate secretly among party members. Also, many of the Old Bolsheviks were still alive, some in positions of power. Stalin knew that many of these men actually hated him, though at the same time they flattered him, and a majority of the Politburo or the Central Committee could still force any one member out of office. Normally calm, almost phlegmatic, Stalin began to show signs of great nervous tension.

In 1932 the leaders of the Communist party celebrated the fifteenth anniversary of their revolution. One of the parties was given by Voroshilov, a Russian general, and attended by Stalin and his young wife Nadezhda. Nadezhda's father had been one of the Old Bolsheviks. All her life she had been taught that communism would benefit mankind. Now, however, as the First Five-Year Plan drew to a close, she was beginning to have doubts.

At this time Russia was desperately short of chemists, engineers, and other technically trained persons who might help the nation speed its industrialization. Determined to help her country, Nadezhda had been studying engineering at the university under an assumed name. Since the students did not know who she was, she sometimes heard things no one would have dared say knowingly to Stalin's wife.

Even among themselves the students were afraid to talk openly. But there were whispers about the vast number of peasants being starved, the men and women dying in the labor camps. Sometimes when Nadezhda heard of an official who had suddenly disappeared because he was suspected of treason, she would remember a remark her husband had made that seemed unimportant at the time but now took on a sinister meaning. Gradually the fear in the back of her mind grew into a certainty—she was living with a monster, a man who had perverted the ideals of communism in his lust for personal power.

She must have been thinking of this on the night of November 8, 1932, when she rode with Stalin to Voroshilov's party. Stalin himself was in a gay mood. Normally he did not drink heavily; he liked to give liquor to other men while he stayed sober, listening to the things they said and storing them away in his mind to use later against the speakers. But this night he drank freely, and though usually a cold man with little interest in women, he began to flirt with one of the ladies.

They were eating dinner when suddenly Nadezhda could stand it no longer. She turned violently on Stalin. "You don't really love your country!" she cried. "You would murder half the people in Russia for your own gain! The only person you love is yourself!"

For a moment there was a shocked silence in the big room. No one dared speak. Then Stalin leaped to his feet, his face contorted with fury. He struck Nadezhda in the face. He shook her violently, screaming curses. Perhaps he would have killed her at that moment, but she broke away from him and ran.

In the dining room people sat as if frozen. Then Voroshilov, the host, stood up and quietly followed Nadezhda. He found her outside and drove her home.

Joseph Stalin's wife Nadezhda (left) just before her death, and young Svetlana with her famous father

It was about one o'clock in the morning when he left her at her door.

Before daylight Nadezhda was dead, with a pistol bullet in her head. It is probable that she committed suicide. It is possible that Joseph Stalin murdered her when he returned home later in the night. Even today the exact truth is unknown. At the time Russian newspapers said she had died of a ruptured appendix.

Whether Stalin actually murdered his wife or simply drove her to suicide, he was certainly responsible for her death. And her death affected him deeply. For years he could not bring himself even to mention her name to his children. Instead, he began to show more affection for his daughter Svetlana. He called her "my little housekeeper," and when he was away on business he wrote her notes signed, "Your little Poppa."

As conditions grew worse in Russia, a few of the Old Bolsheviks dared to speak out against Stalin's rule. Russians who had dreamed that communism would create a heaven on earth were seeing their country turned instead into a kind of hell. Even in the Politburo and the Central Committee there was increased grumbling. Trotsky, who was out of the country and carefully guarded by his own followers, was beyond Stalin's reach. But his letters were being smuggled into Russia demanding a new revolution.

It was a situation Stalin could not tolerate. Besides,

there was still another and extremely important reason for his fear. In 1933 Adolph Hitler came to power in Germany, and quietly began to build a powerful German army. Stalin felt certain that Hitler planned to start a war. But with whom? The capitalist nations had never been friendly with Communist Russia. Always suspicious, Stalin was afraid England and France would actually help Germany rearm, on the condition that Hitler then turn his armies against Russia.

Under these circumstances Stalin must have remembered how the Russian people used the chaos of World War I to overthrow the government of the tsar. In case of another war, what would happen to his own government? Would some of the Old Bolsheviks who were still around use this chance to turn on him? A new revolution could only be staged by one or several of the old recognized leaders. Yet these same leaders were the only persons in Russia that Stalin could not simply order arrested and shot. These men could not be arrested until they had been expelled from the party, and this took a two-thirds vote of two large committees. Stalin controlled both committees, but he was not sure of a two-thirds vote.

He made his plans with care as always. First, he wanted to make sure it was not Great Stalin or even the Communist party that was blamed for the continuing threat of famine or the mistakes in industrialization.

To do this he ordered a group of engineers arrested. After being tortured, they publicly "confessed" that they had sabotaged the industrial program. They had wrecked machinery, built factories that were no good, allowed workers to starve, they said, because they were being paid by foreign nations to ruin the Communist program. The newspapers called them "wreckers" and "enemies of the working class."

But one group of supposed traitors was not enough. Soon other groups were arrested, tortured, and forced to "confess." At the same time, one by one, Stalin was attacking all the Old Bolsheviks he could. Under torture, hoping to save their own lives, the "wreckers and enemies of the working class" would name party leaders who were supposed to have helped them. And these leaders in turn would be eliminated.

It is, of course, probably true that many of these Old Bolsheviks were opposed to Stalin's policies. In democratic countries they could have been members of Congress or Parliament free to express their views. But under communism there was little freedom to disagree. As rapidly as possible Stalin purged (which usually meant killed, jailed, or sent off to Siberia) all those who expressed any disagreement. The men he put in their places were picked to follow him blindly. As a result his control, even over the Old Bolsheviks, was almost total. But for him that was not enough.

In December 1934 a man named Sergey Mironovich Kirov was murdered in Leningrad. Kirov was supposed to be Stalin's closest friend.

Stalin rushed to Leningrad to take over the investigation of the murder. Weeping openly, he blamed Kirov's death on the "wreckers and enemies of the working class."

It now seems almost certain that Stalin himself had plotted Kirov's murder. He did not fire the actual shot any more than he had thrown the bombs in the Tiflis robbery many years before. His method always was to have someone else do the actual deed. But by blaming the death of Kirov, who was probably the most popular of all the Bolshevik leaders, on anti-Communists, Stalin was able to create a great emotional storm within the party and the whole nation. In order to catch and destroy the "enemies of the working class," the secret police were given power to arrest party leaders without a two-thirds vote of any committee. And Stalin, of course, gave the orders to the police.

What followed was one of the strangest and most horrible periods in human history. Men like Kamenev and Zinoviev, who had already been expelled from the party and were totally without power, were re-arrested and charged with incredible lists of crimes: they had planned to murder Lenin, to murder Stalin, and they had never honestly been Communists, but had secretly worked to destroy communism and the Russian government. The entire capitalist world outside Russia, Stalin said, wanted to destroy communism. Capitalist countries had bribed some Communists to turn traitor. Such traitors, no matter what their position within the party, must be exterminated to the last man, Stalin said.

The trials that followed were staged like great theatrical shows. The prisoners were not only tortured to be sure they confessed, they were taught what they were supposed to say. Men who believed totally in communism, who had suffered and worked for it since childhood, stood in open court and said that actually they had been working all the time for foreign capitalist countries. They confessed to crimes that had never been committed. They begged to be executed.

In open court one Old Bolshevik stated, "We were bandits, assassins, fascists. I thank the prosecutor for having demanded for us the death penalty, the only penalty we deserve."

Another said, "I depart as a traitor to my party, a traitor who should be shot."

Many of the accused had been promised that if they confessed they would be sent to prison but not executed. But having "confessed," they were found guilty with few exceptions, and shot immediately.

Some were promised that if they confessed, their

families would be spared. These promises too were rarely kept.

Yet strange as it may seem, not all who confessed did so because of physical torture or even in hope of saving themselves or their families. There was mental torture as well as physical. To the devout Communist, communism was a religion. They believed that the party itself had to be right, always right, because it was to this they had given their lives. With months of questioning in prison dungeons, they came to believe that any opposition to the party leadership was wrong. And since Stalin was the party leader, it was wrong to oppose him, no matter what he did. Such men took the crimes of the party on themselves so that the party itself would not be blamed.

Stalin was not satisfied merely to destroy everyone who had opposed him in the past. He wanted to eliminate anyone who might possibly oppose him in the future. All power was in his hands now, except the power to quiet his own ever-growing fear that someone might take over from him sometime. Therefore he needed to eliminate anyone he suspected, and he suspected almost everyone.

When Kirov was murdered in 1934, there were 1,966 members of the Communist Party Congress. By 1939 Stalin had arrested 1,108 of them, and practically all these were executed. In 1934 there were 139 members and candidate members of the Central Committee. By 1939 Stalin had executed 98 of them. Even so, these represented only a tiny fraction of the executions sweeping across Russia.

Stalin had turned the secret police into a giant murder machine, and now the machine got out of hand. Many of the secret police were former criminals. Now they were free to arrest and execute anyone they did not like, so long as the victim was called anti-Communist. Hoping to please Stalin, some police officers arrested persons on the slightest suspicion, then forced them to confess to crimes the arresting officer had invented. The victims named other persons who would then be arrested, tortured, and these would name still others in turn. Many prisoners were shot; others disappeared into slave labor camps to die of cold, hunger, and overwork.

The secret police made most of the arrests at night, so all night long police vans passed back and forth through the dark streets. No man or woman could go to sleep without fear of a knock on the door. No one could wake in the morning without wondering which of his friends had disappeared during the night. And if a friend had been arrested, if he were being tortured, would he cry out your name in hope of relief?

It was as if death fed on death. There were police officers who came to believe that the more people they destroyed, the better their own chances of promotion. From the headquarters of the secret police in Moscow, orders went to other cities to execute a hundred, a thousand persons—not even names, just numbers. One telegram to the police in Frunze read: "You are charged with exterminating 10,000 enemies of the people. Report results by signal."

Stalin himself took no physical part in these arrests or executions. He did not even attend the great, theatrical purge trials. By the flip of a switch on his desk he could, if he wished, hear the screams of people being tortured in the cellars of the Lubyanka prison. He rarely bothered. He knew what was happening, and that was enough. He had put the knife in the back of literally millions, and now he could work quietly at his desk and then go home and go to sleep.

Why did Stalin allow the purges to roar like a destroying avalanche across the nation? Isaac Deutscher, one of the best of Russian historians, has written that Stalin may have believed that war with Germany was inevitable and that in case of war, the Old Bolsheviks might plot against him. Since he felt that only he, Stalin, could save Russia and communism in time of war, he felt justified in purging all those who might challenge his power. "It is not necessary to assume that he acted from sheer cruelty or lust for power," Deutscher wrote. "He may be given the dubious credit of the sincere conviction that what he did served the interests of the revolution and that he alone interpreted those interests aright."

Years later Stalin's daughter, a grown woman, fled Russia and came to the United States where she wrote a book about her life. In it she insisted that Stalin was not insane. And certainly if he was insane, it was a very crafty and cunning type of insanity that not even Winston Churchill, the British prime minister, or President Franklin Roosevelt would be able to recognize when they met him during World War II.

Yet it seems impossible that a sane man could calmly, knowingly allow millions of innocent people to be murdered. It seems far more likely that the American historian George Kennan was correct when he wrote that Stalin truly was a madman, and that deep in his heart he considered all the world his enemy.

10. Stalin and Hitler

Adolph Hitler's rise to power in Germany was partly due to a great financial depression that swept Europe, Britain, and the United States, beginning in the fall of 1929. As money grew short and people lost jobs, many of them also lost faith in the old systems of government and turned to new, more radical systems. In many countries Communist parties, closely affiliated with that in Russia, gained considerable strength. These were referred to as the left wing of politics. At the other extreme was the radical right wing, the Fascist party of Italy and the Nazi party of Germany.

In many ways Hitler, the Nazi leader, and Joseph Stalin were alike. Both had come from humble origins. Both were clever, cunning, ruthless, and both gained absolute personal power. To a certain extent each man admired the other personally. But in the struggle for power in Germany, the Nazi and Communist parties had fought each other. The Nazis heaped abuse on the Communists, and the Communists referred to the Nazis in such terms as "beasts, pirates, and barbarians."

Despite the name calling, Stalin for a while seemed far more interested in his domestic problems than in what was happening in Germany. By the late 1930s, however, it became obvious that Hitler was preparing for war. At the same time he was demanding that parts of Poland and other countries that lay between Germany and Russia be given to Germany. Since German rulers had always envied the rich farmlands of eastern Russia, it seemed likely that Hitler might be planning war on Russia.

At this point Stalin had three roads he might try to take:

1. He might build his own military power while planning to fight alone if necessary. (Stalin knew, however, that at this time Russia was in no condition to fight a war. Time in which to arm was absolutely necessary.)

2. Stalin might try for an alliance with the British and the French; then if Hitler started a war, Germany would have to fight on both an eastern and a western front.

3. Stalin might try to reach some agreement with Hitler so that Russia would be left in peace while Germany turned on England and France.

Because of the conflict and name calling which had gone on between the Nazi and Communist parties, there seemed little chance of reaching an agreement with Hitler. Stalin, therefore, made his first overtures toward the British and the French. These met with little success. For years the Communist parties within England and France had worked to overthrow those governments, so the English and the French did not trust Stalin or communism.

This rebuff made Stalin even more suspicious of the democracies than ever. And when the Allies continued to give in to Hitler, Stalin felt sure England and France were trying to promote a war between Germany and Russia.

There was at least a grain of truth in this. Certainly there were many persons in the British and French governments who would have liked to see the Nazis and Communists destroy each other. At the same time, there was nothing Stalin would have liked better than to see Germany and the Allies batter each other into helplessness, after which he could step in and dictate his own terms.

Cautiously, Stalin made secret advances toward Hitler. At the same time he continued friendly overtures to the British and the French.

As it became obvious that appeasement would not turn Hitler from his course, the Allies looked with more favor on a Russian treaty. Finally they sent a military mission to Moscow to work out such an agreement. Even then, however, neither side really trusted the other. Both sides stalled, and there was little progress.

Meanwhile, Stalin's undercover discussions with Hitler moved faster. On August 23, 1939, Joachim von Ribbentrop, Hitler's foreign minister, arrived secretly in Moscow. That same afternoon he met with Stalin.

Ribbentrop was a rather pompous, conceited man. He knew Hitler had no intention of keeping an agreement one moment longer than it suited him, and he felt sure that he and Hitler were making a fool of Stalin.

Stalin, on his part, never forgot an insult and had no intention of forgetting those that had been heaped on him by the Germans. But he could put on an act, and now he looked a little shy, almost embarrassed as he shook hands with Ribbentrop. "Well," he said, "we certainly have been cursing each other for a long time."

Ribbentrop made a grand gesture. "That was political talk with no meaning," he said. "The truth is that Chancellor Hitler admires you and the Russian people tremendously."

Stalin smiled and said that he and the Russians admired Hitler. Then with these social graces out of the way, they sat down to serious talk.

The agreement they reached consisted of two parts, but only the first was to be made public at the time.

Stalin and von Ribbentrop shake hands after signing
the German–Russian nonaggression pact.

In this Russia and Germany agreed that neither country
would take any part in a war against the other.

The secret part was more complex. In it they made
detailed plans on how to divide eastern Europe between
them, if war came. And Stalin knew as well as Ribbentrop
that Hitler was about to start a war.

On September 1, 1939, exactly eight days after the
signing of the treaty, German armies invaded Poland.
Two days later Britain and France honored their
promises to come to Poland's help. And World War
II was under way.

Sitting beneath the pictures of Marx and Lenin,
Stalin smoked his pipe and smiled happily. He had
made himself dictator of Russia by setting his opponents

one against another and letting them destroy each other. Now, he hoped, the British–French Allies and the Germans would wipe each other out. Eventually their governments might fall in chaos, Communist parties take over, and Joseph Stalin might rule Europe, maybe the world. At the very least, Stalin had bought precious time in which to improve his own military position.

At first everything seemed to go according to plan. The German army smashed Polish resistance, and Stalin sent his forces in to take over the part of Poland he and Hitler had agreed on. Russian troops also moved into the little Baltic countries of Estonia, Latvia, and Lithuania. These nations were too small even to fight back. Then Stalin called on Finland to surrender the part of its territory that was close to the Russian border and to the city of Leningrad. This would make any future defense of the area easier. But to Stalin's surprise, the Finns refused.

Stalin tried masked threats, then open ones. But the Finns remained stubborn, and eventually Stalin realized they were not going to give in. Even so, he did not want to declare war on a small country without any excuse other than the demand for territory. He made his plans with care. One morning seven artillery shells fell on a Russian village near the Finnish border. Nobody has ever been able to prove where the shells came from. But with great indignation Stalin cried out that tiny Finland had attacked Russia, and he sent his army crashing across the border.

At this point things began to go wrong. In Stalin's purge of the Russian leaders, many of the best military men had been murdered. Now the Russian army was poorly led. And the Finns fought like fiends. For a brief time it looked as if the tiny Finnish army might actually win. Then the tremendous weight of Russian manpower took over. The Finns were forced to surrender the part of their country Stalin wanted, and Russia and Finland made an uneasy peace.

Soon Stalin was in for another surprise. Although Britain and France had declared war on Germany, they had not done much actual fighting. Now with Poland conquered, Hitler turned his armies west, and in the spring of 1940 hurled them against France. With amazing speed they crushed the French army; France surrendered and Britain was left alone. But Britain was protected by the English Channel. Faced by the powerful British fleet, Hitler decided not to attempt an invasion of Great Britain immediately.

Stalin was shocked by the tremendous power of the German army. He had expected the Germans and the Allies to batter each other to pieces. Now instead of a weak and exhausted Germany on his western border, he had Hitler in command of the world's most powerful army. And Hitler, in full command of western Europe, but blocked by the English Channel, had no way to go except east—toward Russia.

For generations German rulers had envied those areas of southern Russia that produced great quantities of foodstuffs. Now it seemed certain to most of the world that Hitler would ignore the treaty he had signed with Stalin and attack Russia.

Exactly what Stalin believed is uncertain. Several times he told his generals they should expect war with Hitler in the late fall of 1941 or the spring of 1942, but not before then. At other times he told them Hitler would not attack at all. He worked to put his nation on a war footing, but without any great hurry. The one thing he seemed absolutely sure of was that if Hitler did attack, the attack would not come before the fall of 1941.

It was about this same time that one of Stalin's agents finally managed to murder Leon Trotsky. Trotsky was living in Mexico, and the murderer gained admission to his house by posing as a friend. While Trotsky worked at his desk, writing a biography of Joseph Stalin, the killer slipped up behind him and struck him on the head with an ax. Stalin could now turn his energy toward preparing Russia for war, secure in the knowledge that the last of his rivals was dead.

In England Winston Churchill, the British prime minister, learned from spies that Hitler was massing many of his troops along the Russian border. He sent a message to Stalin warning him of this.

Stalin also had messages from his own men inside Germany. Hitler's finest troops were moving east. Tanks and planes were moving east. Huge quantities of war supplies were being stored near the Russian border.

Probably no government has had a more complete warning of an attack planned against it. Why Stalin simply refused to act on this warning, no one can say with certainty. He mobilized part of his army, but not all. Apparently he remained certain that Hitler could not attack before the autumn of 1941.

Hitler, however, did not wait. Before dawn of June 22 German armies burst across the Russian frontier. From the Baltic Sea in the north to the Black Sea in the south, the invasion rolled forward.

Stalin was in his office and it was nearing dawn, about the time he usually went to bed, when the reports began to reach him. German planes were bombing Russian cities. They were attacking Russian ships.

Still Stalin would not believe it. These were merely a few undisciplined German units that were trying to cause trouble, he said. Hitler would not have ordered a full-fledged invasion.

More reports poured in. German troops had crossed the border along a tremendous front. These were not small units; these were armies. Russian commanders phoned, wired, begged for orders. They could not reach Stalin, and no one else knew what to say.

The invasion began before dawn, but it was noon before Molotov, the Russian foreign minister, told the people, "The Soviet Government and its head, Comrade Stalin, have instructed me to make the following announcement: At 4:00 A.M. without declaration of war and without any claims being made, German troops attacked our country." Russian soldiers, he said, "have been ordered to repulse the predatory attack." Then he begged the people "to rally around the glorious Bolshevik Party, around the Soviet Government, and our great leader, Comrade Stalin."

And Great Stalin, Father of Peoples, the military genius who had assured his country the Germans would not yet attack—where was he? All over Russia people stared at one another and wondered.

Years later after Stalin's death, Ivan Maisky, the Soviet ambassador to London, gave an answer. Soon after the attack began, the ambassador said, Joseph Stalin had locked himself in a room with a bottle. He became too drunk to give orders. He could not yet face the fact that Hitler had made a fool of him, that he had put his judgement above that of all the people who had tried to warn him, and that he had been wrong. To members of the Politburo he wept, "All that Lenin built, we have lost."

11. World War II

For several days Stalin was in a state of shock that bordered on a complete mental breakdown. During all this time the great Russian nation lay leaderless, almost helpless. Under Stalin's dictatorship there had been no vice-president, no man who dared step in and take control. The few orders that did go out from the Kremlin were confused, uncertain. And the German army, meeting almost no opposition, was advancing into Russia at a rate of twenty miles a day.

Gradually Stalin got control of himself. He was the leader of his country, and something had to be done. On July 3, eleven days after the invasion began, he spoke over the radio to the Russian people.

"Comrades, citizens, brothers and sisters." His voice was strained, hesitant. "Men of the army and navy. I am addressing you, my friends."

It was the first time he had ever spoken this way. Only a short time before he had been ordering a bloody purge of many of these same "brothers and sisters" and "friends." Now it was different. Now he needed help.

At the same time he knew, as he had always known, that the Russian people—at least those who knew anything about him—did not love him. Many did not love the Communist party. And so Stalin shrewdly spoke to them of his own love of Russia, and of their love of their native land. It was not communism they must fight for, but Russia, the motherland.

It was a clever appeal and eventually it had effect, but it took time. When the German armies first moved into Russia, many Russians defended their country bravely. On the other hand, thousands upon thousands of other Russian troops cheerfully surrendered. In some cases, entire villages met the invaders with smiles and flowers, happy to be rid of Communist rule.

The Germans themselves, acting largely under Hitler's orders, soon changed this. They not only treated the Russians as an inferior, second-class people, but often met them with barbarous savagery. They burned towns, executed captured Russian officers, and allowed other prisoners to starve by the thousands. Peasants who had hoped the German invasion would mean the end of the collective farms found they were forced to remain on the farms and to work like slaves. Many Russians who had cheerfully welcomed the Germans soon turned against them. They began to fight for their homeland with an almost incredible fury.

In England, Winston Churchill made a speech saying

Great Britain would help the Soviet Union in every way possible against Hitler, their common enemy. Stalin, as usual, was suspicious. But everyday the German armies were moving closer to Leningrad and to Moscow, and in desperation Stalin asked for help. He not only wanted tanks and planes, he wanted a British army to land in France. This would have forced Germany to fight on two fronts at the same time.

Churchill tried to explain that England had been fighting Germany for one year completely alone and simply did not have the strength to open new fronts at this time. Stalin insisted. He had no knowledge of naval affairs and of the number of ships necessary to do what he asked. Later Churchill wrote that "it seemed hopeless to argue with a man thinking in terms of utter unreality."

At this time the United States was still at peace, but President Roosevelt also offered vast quantities of supplies to aid the Russians. In late July he sent Harry L. Hopkins to discuss with Stalin what was needed.

By this time Stalin was once more in full command of himself. He wore a plain uniform very much like the ones he had been wearing for years. He was calm, confident of final victory. But he was also deadly serious. He recognized the power of the German army. "Our losses have been tremendous," he told Hopkins. "They still are. But if you give us antiaircraft guns—20,000

One of the most savage battles of the war was fought
at Stalingrad. Crushing air attacks and bitter house-
to-house fighting forced women and children to hide
in caves and basements.

antiaircraft guns—and aluminum for our factories, we can fight on for three or four years."

Harry Hopkins was accustomed to dealing with great men, including President Roosevelt and Winston Churchill; even so, he was tremendously impressed with Stalin. Later he wrote that Stalin "shook my hand briefly, warmly, courteously. He smiled warmly. There was no waste of word, gesture, or mannerism. It was like talking to a perfectly coordinated machine, an intelligent machine."

However, when Hopkins talked with other members of the Russian government, he caught a glimpse of another side of Stalin. Hopkins had come to Russia to find what its army needed so the United States could send help. But no general, no Russian official, dared tell him anything. Hopkins asked General Yakovlev, "What's the size of the largest Russian tank?"

The general coughed. He rubbed his fingers nervously across his chin. Finally he said, "It's a good tank."

"Do you need more tanks?" Hopkins asked. "More antitank guns?"

The general fidgeted in his chair, looking miserable. "I'm not empowered to say whether or not we need these things," he said.

Hopkins went back to Stalin, and Stalin, he learned, had a remarkable mind for details and numbers. He knew exactly how many tanks and planes Russia had.

He knew the weight of the tanks, the speed of the planes, and the size of the guns. He spoke rapidly, frankly telling Hopkins what was needed. But under the system of terror by which he ruled, no other person in Russia dared give an answer.

Hopkins went back to report to President Roosevelt. Meanwhile the German army continued to drive deeper and deeper into Russia. Stalin had already appointed himself head of the government as premier. Despite all his years as dictator, this was his first official government office. Now he also made himself supreme commander of the armed forces.

Stalin's exact role in the gigantic struggle is still uncertain. Until the time of his death, everything published in Russia praised him not only as a leader who inspired the Russian people, but as a tremendous military genius. Years later Nikita Khrushchev in a speech before the Communist Party Congress told another story. On one occasion, Khrushchev said, the Germans were driving toward the city of Kharkov when Stalin ordered a counterattack. Before this could happen, German forces cut through the Russian lines.

Stalin had gone to a country house just outside Moscow while the battle was going on. He was there when the phone rang and G. M. Malenkov, one of his assistants, answered. Malenkov listened for a while, then turned to Stalin. "It's Comrade Khrushchev," he said. "He's with the troops near Kharkov and wants to talk with you."

Stalin already had reports that the battle was not going well. "Tell Nikita you will take the message," Stalin said.

Malenkov then repeated this to Khrushchev, but Khrushchev was desperate. "Tell Comrade Stalin I must talk with him. He is the only one who can change the orders."

Malenkov did not like being caught in the middle. He looked unhappily at Stalin. "Comrade—"

"Tell him you will take the report," Stalin said.

Nikita Khrushchev at the front in Stalingrad with some of the troops under his command

Once more Malenkov repeated Stalin's words, and Khrushchev, who knew there was no use arguing and did not dare do so anyway, explained to Malenkov the military situation: The Russian attack had been broken into fragments. To continue the attack would waste the lives of thousands of men without stopping the German advance. It was best to retreat, reform the troops, and attack again from another position. "Take a map," Khrushchev pleaded. "Show Stalin the situation. Get him to order a retreat."

"Hold the line," Malenkov said. Then he repeated to Stalin what Khrushchev had said.

Stalin listened, smoking his pipe. When Malenkov had finished he said, "Let everything remain as it is," and turned away.

That was it. No one dared argue, not even the commanding generals on the scene.

In his speech to the Communist Party Congress after Stalin's death, Khrushchev asked, "And what was the result of Stalin's order? The worst that we had expected. The Germans surrounded our army concentrations, and consequently we lost hundreds of thousands of our soldiers. This is Stalin's military 'genius'; this is what it cost us."

At the time of this speech, Khrushchev had personal reasons for wanting to destroy Stalin's reputation. His story may or may not have been exactly true. Certainly

Stalin's cold mind had no more regard for the lives of soldiers than he had had for the lives of the kulaks, and he threw troops into battle as if shoveling coal into a furnace. On the other hand, he had an extraordinary ability to remember and use figures and details. Although his decision was final on every point, he usually listened carefully to his generals and often, though not always, took their advice.

Stalin was cautious about risking his personal reputation. In the early days of the war with the fighting going against Russia, Stalin gave the orders but had practically all of them signed by Marshal Shaposhnikov, the chief of staff. If there had to be a scapegoat later, it would be the marshal, not Stalin.

The early German advance moved so swiftly that by the middle of October 1941, it looked as though Moscow itself would be captured. Stalin ordered factories taken apart piece by piece and shipped east, away from the Germans. Everyone who was not needed for defense was sent away. Stalin stayed on. A special air-raid shelter was built for him inside the Kremlin. It was more than 100 feet deep, with steel-lined corridors and thick steel doors. Here he spent most of his time, and from here the orders went to the various fronts to fight and keep fighting.

From the first, Stalin realized that any hope of final victory must depend largely on two things: supplies and the will of the people to fight. Russia could not manufacture enough of the machines of war to defeat Germany, but Britain and the United States were helping. There remained the will of the people. And Stalin in his radio speeches shrewdly played not on a love of communism, but on a love of country. Over and over he spoke of the sacrifices the Russian people had made for their motherland in the past. Ancient heroes whom the Bolsheviks had not mentioned for years, except to attack them for having served under the tsars, were suddenly heroes again. Whereas in the past Stalin had tried to abolish religion, he now allowed many churches to reopen and asked the priests to pray for their country.

In his speeches Stalin did not always worry too much about the truth. He quoted Hitler as having written: "Man is sinful from the moment of his birth and can be ruled only by force. . . . When politics require it, it is necessary to lie, betray, and even kill." It was a statement with which both Stalin and Hitler might well have agreed, but Hitler had never written it.

In this same speech Stalin said that 4,500,000 German soldiers had been killed in battle, while only 350,000 Russian soldiers had fallen. He was simply making the figures up; they had nothing to do with the truth. But they made the people feel better.

There can be no doubt that in these speeches Stalin did much to raise the morale of the Russian people.

When the German armies came within a few miles of Moscow, most of the Communist officials fled east. Stalin remained, and the fact that he was there cheered the people. It gave them hope of victory, and they fought the Germans with a savage and desperate fury. Not only the young men, thousands upon thousands of women went into the army. Old men, women, and children dug huge ditches in which to trap the German tanks. In temperatures far below zero they carried ammunition, loaded and unloaded trains, worked the clock around in unheated factories. In territory occupied by the Germans, they formed guerrilla bands to attack the supply trains, and to destroy bridges and roads.

Probably no people in history have fought more valiantly against an invader than did the Russians.

12. Stalin, Churchill, and Roosevelt

On December 7, 1941, Japanese planes bombed Pearl Harbor. Germany and Italy then joined Japan in a declaration of war against the United States, and World War II had become worldwide indeed.

In Moscow Stalin listened with grim pleasure to the news. German armies were still driving deeper into Russia, but now that the United States, Great Britain, and Russia all were fighting together, there was a much better chance of victory than before. Stalin immediately renewed his demands for a second front against Hitler.

Both Roosevelt and Churchill tried by telegrams and diplomatic messages to explain the situation to Stalin. Most of the American ships and landing craft had to go to the Pacific for the war against Japan. There were simply not enough left over to stage an invasion of western Europe at this time. But Stalin kept insisting, and in August 1942 Churchill flew to Moscow to explain things in person to the Russian dictator.

The two men were strangely alike, yet vastly different. Both were short, heavyset. Churchill was a British aristocrat, but he believed totally in democracy and willingly

Stalin accompanies Churchill to the airport at the conclusion of their meeting in Moscow.

recognized the limitations of his office as a prime minister who might be dismissed at any time by the British Parliament. Stalin was the son of Georgian serfs and had made himself dictator. He had always hated the British, and Churchill on his part had hated and opposed communism ever since the October Revolution of 1917. Now they represented allies who had nothing in common, except that both were in a life-and-death struggle with Hitler.

The meeting was formal. Neither man spoke the language of the other, and everything had to be translated by an interpreter. Churchill explained the shortage of shipping. At this time, he said, the British and Americans could send perhaps five or six divisions across the English Channel into France, but such a small force would be quickly defeated. This would not help Russia, and it would hurt the general war effort.

Stalin listened, frowning. "Hitler has no good troops in France," he said. "Five or six British divisions could hold a beachhead and force Hitler to withdraw troops from the Russian front."

"Hitler has twenty-five divisions in France," Churchill told him. "And nine of them are excellent."

Stalin shook his head. He knew Churchill was right, but he would not admit it. Instead he asked insultingly, "Why are you British and Americans so afraid of the Germans? Why do you refuse to fight?"

Churchill held his temper. "Have you ever asked yourself why Hitler did not invade England after the fall of France? He was at the peak of his power. Britain had lost nearly all her supplies in the retreat from France. Yet Hitler stopped at the Channel. The English Channel is not so easy to cross."

Stalin shrugged. He knew very little about ships and the demands of sea warfare, but he knew a lot about men. He realized that he could push this short, roly-poly Englishman just so far without losing more in the argument than he had gained. So he dropped it.

Churchill then explained that although Britain and the

United States could not at that time invade France, they could send troops into North Africa, which was not so heavily fortified. This would force Hitler to transfer troops and aircraft from the Russian front.

Stalin's face changed. Eagerly he leaned over the map Churchill had spread on the table. And now his quick understanding impressed Churchill exactly as it had impressed Harry Hopkins the year before. Later Churchill would write, "Very few people alive could have comprehended the situation in so few minutes. . . . He saw it all in a flash."

That night Joseph Stalin was smiling and pleasant when the meeting with Churchill broke up. But next morning he was once more surly and insulting, asking why the British were afraid to attack the Germans in France. Once again, however, he changed his tone the moment he decided he had gone as far as he safely dared.

It was true that at this time Russia bore the main burden of the war against Germany. But in the next months British and American troops did drive the Germans and Italians out of North Africa. They invaded Italy. Their aircraft dropped a constant rain of bombs on Germany, and their ships carried an ever-increasing flow of supplies to Russia.

This was never enough for Stalin. He was constantly demanding more, and his demands annoyed Churchill more than they did President Roosevelt, who at this time had not met the Russian dictator. In his conversations with Churchill, the president always referred to Stalin as "Uncle Joe." He felt sure that Uncle Joe was really a rather decent person despite his gruffness. Churchill was far more dubious.

In October 1943, Churchill sent a telegram to Stalin promising four more convoys of supplies as soon as possible. Stalin answered angrily that he wanted them now; it was the absolute obligation of Britain and the United States to send them, he said.

The tone of the answer was a bit too much for Churchill. He sent a copy of it to Roosevelt along with a note, saying "I have now received a telegram from Uncle Joe which I think you will feel is not exactly all one might hope for from a gentleman for whose sake we are to make an inconvenient, extreme, and costly exertion. . . . I think, or at least I hope, this message came from the machine rather than Stalin. . . . The Soviet machine is quite convinced it can get everything by bullying."

Churchill was right, except that the Soviet machine and Stalin were very much the same thing.

It was about this time that the tide of war began to change in Russia. The German advance stopped, then broke into retreat. All along a front that stretched for hundreds of miles, the Russians drove forward.

And it was about this time that Stalin began to sign most of the orders that came out of the Kremlin. He had always given them, but in the days of defeat he had had someone else sign them. Now that victory seemed more certain, he made sure he got the credit.

There had long been a need for the leaders of the three most powerful allies to get together personally. In late November 1943, Stalin, Roosevelt, and Churchill met at Teheran, the capital city of Iran.

It was a convenient location for Stalin, only one day's flight from Moscow. But for both Roosevelt and Churchill it was a long and difficult journey. They had agreed to the meeting place only because Stalin insisted that he could not go far away from the war.

In his telegrams to the other leaders, Stalin frequently wrote, "I am leaving for the front," or "I have just returned from the front," or "I have been a long time at the front."

Actually, if he ever visited the front at all, there is no record of it. Instead, he spent most of the war in Moscow, not because he was afraid, but because as commander-in-chief he was far more valuable in his headquarters than he would have been with the troops. Yet as Bukharin had once said, "Djugashvili can't live if he doesn't have what someone else has." Stalin was not satisfied to be commander—he had to make it look as if he were fighting the war single-handedly.

By now Stalin had promoted himself to be a marshal of the Red army, and instead of a plain uniform, he wore a fancy one with huge red stars on the shoulders. In his dealing with Churchill and Roosevelt, he was as cunning and shrewd as ever. When Churchill asked, "What territory will Russia insist on controlling after the war?" Stalin brushed the question aside.

"There is no need to speak at the present about any Soviet desires," he said. "But when the time comes, we will speak."

Both Roosevelt and Churchill asked for a better answer. Stalin answered that Russia would want security, that was all. "We must make sure that Germany cannot start another war."

Everyone agreed on that. But, Roosevelt asked, what about the smaller nations along the Russian frontier: Poland, Romania, Czechoslovakia? Would Russia allow them free elections to determine their own form of government?

"Of course," Stalin said. "The Soviet Union wants them to be friendly, but free and independent." He repeated the promise several times, smiling, agreeable —and very probably without the slightest intention of keeping his word.

This conference ended in December 1943. A few months later, in the early spring, Stalin launched a giant offensive against the Germans. Losses were terrible on both sides, but the Russians pushed steadily westward. Then in June, British and American armies crossed the

The three leaders met again at Yalta in 1945. Seated
left to right are Churchill, Roosevelt, and Stalin.

English Channel. In bloody fighting they crossed France
and swept into Germany from the west.

By February 1945 it was obvious that Hitler could
not hold out much longer. Once more Stalin, Roosevelt,
and Churchill met, this time at the Russian city of Yalta.
Sitting around a big table littered with maps, they
planned the future boundaries of European nations.

When Roosevelt arrived in Yalta, he was already a
sick man, not capable of a battle of wits with Joseph
Stalin. Also, he still believed that Stalin would keep any
promises he made. Though Stalin insisted on gaining
territory for Russia, he did promise time and again that

he would allow the small nations along his border to be free and independent.

He did not keep this promise for long. As the Russian army occupied one country after another in eastern Europe, Stalin drew what Churchill called an "iron curtain" around them. He refused even to allow American or British officials to visit and find out what was happening. And instead of letting the people hold free, independent elections, he set up Communist governments he could control as totally as he controlled Russia.

In the White House in Washington, one month before his death, President Roosevelt was reading reports from Europe. As he read his face grew pale. "Stalin can't be trusted!" he said. "He's broken his word on every promise he made to me at Yalta!"

13. Terror Comes Home

By the spring of 1945 Hitler's armies had been crushed. On the last day of April, Hitler himself committed suicide, and a week later one of his generals signed the official surrender. The war in the Pacific continued for another three months, then Japan too surrendered.

Of all the important war leaders, only Stalin remained in power after the war was over. Roosevelt, overworked and exhausted, died of a stroke. Mussolini was murdered by his own people. Hitler committed suicide. And Winston Churchill was voted out of office by a British people weary of war.

In Russia there were no free elections, and Joseph Stalin remained in absolute control. He was sixty-six years old now. His hair was white, his face a little thinner, the lines deeper. He looked almost benevolent, and to the great majority of the Russian people, inspired by the stories of his war-time leadership, he seemed not only majestic but truly godlike.

He still had no idea of the value of money because he never spent any. He lived surrounded by an army of servants furnished by the government. Anything he wanted was immediately brought to him. But his tastes were still simple. He had no desire for luxury, except for one thing. This was a desire for country houses, called *dachas*. He had them built for him all over Russia but even these were basically simple, very much alike, and not luxurious by American standards.

When Stalin went from one dacha to another, he went by special train. Another armed train went ahead to clear the way. Soldiers lined the tracks. If the train stopped at a station, the station was cleared of people, and no one was allowed near. Then Stalin might step down, walk the length of the train, and talk for a few moments with the engineer. But the engineers were too awed to do more than mumble, and Stalin would walk back to his armored car and climb aboard again—the most powerful man in the world, lonely and always afraid.

Once on a trip to his native Georgia, the peasants were allowed to meet the train. These were people who knew nothing of Stalin except that he was supposed to be responsible for every good thing in the world and none of the bad. They came in great crowds, bringing presents of fruit and bottles of wine to give him. They surrounded the train, cheering.

Stalin grew furious. He did not want to be bothered, and besides, he did not trust crowds. His daughter

Svetlana, a grown woman now, was with him. He turned on her as if she were responsible. "Fools!" he shouted. "They are all fools!" He ordered the train to back up and left the people staring at one another.

Then Stalin turned on the generals and the government officials who were with him, cursing them viciously. They did not dare answer, and gradually his rage cooled. A servant brought him a bottle of wine, and Stalin thanked him pleasantly, sincerely.

This was one of the many strange quirks of Stalin's character. He was nearly always polite with the servants who waited on him—the cooks, maids, the men who worked in the gardens of his many dachas. From them he had nothing to fear. They offered no threat to his power or to his safety, and with them he could be not only polite, but even friendly. If there was anyone, anywhere, who both knew and loved Joseph Stalin, it must have been these servants who waited on him.

With the high government officials who surrounded him, it was a different matter. Stalin knew well that, with possibly one or two exceptions, the men he had promoted and kept in power both feared and hated him and one another. Even during the war they had watched one another with jealousy, suspicion, and hatred. When Stalin had someone else sign his orders while the Russians were losing battles, it set a precedent many other officials followed, each trying to find someone else to take the blame. Stalin knew they followed him now like a pack of jackals after an aging lion.

The more carefully Stalin studied the men around him, the more he feared them. They had known and been friendly with many of the people he had destroyed in the past. Did they hate him now because of what he had done? Even if they did not hate him, they had been willing to accept murder to advance their own careers, so certainly they could not be trusted. Therefore he watched the men closest to him with steadily growing fear and hate. There were times when he took savage pleasure in cursing and humiliating the leaders who, after him, were the most powerful in the Soviet Union.

With the end of the war many persons had begun to whisper that now, with the nation at peace, there ought to be more liberty. Stalin did not see it that way. Russia was no longer closely encircled by capitalist nations. Poland, Romania, and the other countries along Russia's western border were now Communist, dominated by Moscow. But Stalin was still fearful. The only way to make Russia safe, he said, was to make it more powerful. He devised a new Five-Year Plan, and once more the weary people were sent to labor camps and forced into bigger and bigger collective farms.

In all this work, emphasis was placed on materials that could be used in war. In a remarkably short time, Russia greatly increased its production of steel, coal, and electricity. The first Russian atom bomb was exploded. Russia became, next to the United States, the most powerful and scientifically advanced nation in the world.

There were, however, very few comforts for the Russian people. There was still a shortage of food and clothing. Housing was so short that it was common for two, sometimes even three or four, families to share one small apartment.

There were few complaints because the Russian people were both too weary and fearful to complain. Even so, in 1948 Stalin began a new purge. Exactly what he hoped to accomplish and what his own personal terrors were at this time are uncertain. But once more people were arrested by the thousands and tens of thousands. They were accused of spying for the British, the Americans, of having spied for Germany, of being anti-Communist. As before, most of the arrests were made at night, the police vans racing through the dark streets of Moscow, Leningrad, and other cities until dawn. Once more people awoke wondering which of their friends had disappeared during the night, and whose turn would be next.

Years before, Stalin had ordered the arrest and murder of some of his wife's male relatives. Now he had her sister and sister-in-law arrested, tortured, and put in solitary confinement. His daughter Svetlana came to him in tears, the only one who dared approach him.

"Papa, what has happened to Aunt Anna and Aunt Yevgenia? Why have they been arrested? Why?"

He glared at her. "They talked too much. They knew too much, and they talked. It helped our enemies."

"But papa, they—" His face stopped her, and she knew it was hopeless. Once Stalin had decided someone was an enemy, no matter how flimsy the evidence, he simply refused to change his mind.

Years later, after Stalin's death, Svetlana's aunts were released from prison. One had gone mad in solitary confinement. The other, gaunt and gray, admitted she had signed all kinds of false confessions—she had claimed to be a spy, to having poisoned her husband, to have plotted against Stalin. "In your father's prisons," she told Svetlana, "a person will sign anything just to be left alone and not tortured. All night in prison you could hear persons screaming in agony, begging to be killed."

Many of the persons arrested in this purge were Jews, and often for no reason except that they were Jews. Stalin had always been somewhat anti-Jewish. As he grew older, this feeling turned to a reasonless hatred.

In 1949 Joseph Stalin was seventy years old. As on his fiftieth birthday, the servile officials surrounding him decided it would please the old man to have a great celebration. In nearly every city, not only in Russia, but in the conquered countries of eastern Europe, huge statues were erected. Millions of small statues were made and given to the people. It was dangerous for any office, any home not to have a statue, or at least a big picture of Stalin hung on the wall.

Once more Communist officials rivaled one another to see who could say the most wonderful things about Great Stalin. The government newspaper announced that soon the whole world would celebrate Stalin's birthday, and the world calendar would start, not with the birth of Christ, but with the birth of Stalin.

One official wrote: "Hundreds and millions of peoples in all the countries of the world, and all progressive mankind, see in Comrade Stalin their beloved leader and teacher, and they believe and know that the cause of Lenin and Stalin is invincible."

Another wrote: "In all languages of the peoples of the world, the words of greeting to our leader: 'Glory to Comrade Stalin! Forward to new victories under the leadership of Great Stalin.'"

Stalin took it all with a curious mixture of faith and cynicism. He believed that the praise was just and due. At the same time, he knew that many of the men who praised him most loudly truly hated him.

He was publishing his *Collected Works*, often rewriting and changing his old speeches and articles to make it look as if he had foreseen the future. He wrote a history of communism in which he referred to himself as "the sublime military stategist of all time."

But fear was in his veins. It had always been there and now as he grew older, the fear grew stronger. He trusted no one, so there was no one he could talk to, no one he could believe. The men around him whispered about one another, and he believed the worst of all of it. He accused Voroshilov, marshal of the Red army and his closest friend—if he had a friend —of being a spy for the British. He deported the wife of his foreign minister because she was Jewish. He was

At this swimming meet, portraits of "Great Stalin" are floated in the water to prove devotion to the leader.

planning a new purge, perhaps a greater and bloodier purge than any that had gone before it. It would threaten the lives of every government official, and they all knew it. But there was nothing they could do. They mistrusted one another as much as they mistrusted Stalin.

What followed would be known in history as the "doctors' plot."

It began with the arrest of nine of the most famous doctors in Russia. As in the earlier purges, many of these victims were Jewish. They were referred to as the Kremlin doctors because many of their patients had been government officials living in the Kremlin. One was Stalin's own personal doctor.

The secret police, acting under Stalin's orders, announced that the doctors had used "improper techniques" to murder some of their most famous patients. They were accused of having tried to murder others, including admirals and generals. Stalin told Semyon Ignatiev, who headed the state police, "If you don't get confessions, we'll see that you are shortened by a head."

Ignatiev got his confessions from some of the doctors. They signed statements saying they had been spies; they had planned to murder Stalin; they had worked to destroy Russia.

Not all the doctors signed these confessions. Some

160

died under torture rather than confess to these false accusations.

Stalin announced that the doctors would not have been able to commit these crimes if it had not been for the criminal carelessness of Soviet security organizations.

This sent a chill of terror through the top government officials, because it meant that almost anybody could be accused, and probably would be. Some went into hiding. But it was useless to hide from Stalin's police, and they knew it.

The first public announcement of the "doctors' plot" had named nine doctors arrested. Actually there were dozens of others arrested without any announcement. One day they were in their offices; the next day they were gone. No one knew where or why, and no one knew who might be next.

This was the situation on the first of March 1953. Stalin was living in one of his dachas near Moscow. He had quit traveling. He was afraid to travel, even in an armored train surrounded by soldiers, because he did not trust soldiers. At home all the food he ate and even the air in his rooms were tested by chemists for poison. And he did not trust the chemists. He trusted nobody. He stayed in his dacha plotting a bloody purge that would destroy his enemies. And his enemies were everywhere.

He had high blood pressure. He was not well. But he had arrested the one doctor in whom he put any trust at all, and now he had nobody. He needed medical help, but he was afraid.

Exactly what happened we cannot say. Later different Communist officials would tell different stories. It may be that none of them really knew the truth. Joseph Stalin may have been poisoned by some person close to him who was terrified for his own life. It is more likely that Stalin's own fear helped bring on a stroke.

The story in which we can put the most faith is the one told by his daughter Svetlana after she had fled Russia and was living in the United States.

On March 2, 1953 Svetlana was attending class at a graduate school in Moscow when word came that she was wanted at her father's dacha. A chauffeured car was waiting. At the dacha a number of government officials stood just outside the door, and one of them told Svetlana that her father had suffered a stroke. It had happened sometime during the night. He had been alone, but a servant had found him at 3:00 A.M., lying on the floor of his room. He was still alive, but unconscious.

Inside the house Svetlana found her father had been placed on a sofa. He was surrounded by a swarm of doctors and nurses, all of them tense, frightened, but doing their best and knowing already the task was hopeless.

Also present were practically all the top government officials. Nervously they watched one another more than they watched Stalin. Everyone of them knew that once the old dictator was dead, once they were sure he was dead, they would devour one another like sharks in the struggle for his power. But until he died they dared not move.

And whatever the cause, Joseph Stalin took a long time to die. All that day of March second, then the third, the fourth, he lay unmoving. Now and then his eyes would open. The doctors, nurses, the watching officials would halt, stand almost unbreathing. Then Stalin's eyes would close again, and no one knew whether in those moments he had been conscious or not.

Suddenly the old man's eyes were wide open and fully conscious. His gaze swept the room, the doctors, nurses, the government officials, his daughter sitting in a chair close beside him. It was a look half of terror, half of inhuman hatred. He raised his left arm, the hand clawlike, as if he would bring down a curse upon them all, upon the whole world. His face twisted in fury. He tried to speak but no sound came out. And then he died.

For a long moment no one in the room dared move. Slowly a doctor leaned over the body, and stepped back again. Then sure at last that Stalin was dead, the Communist officials turned their backs and raced for the door. The fight for power among Stalin's heirs had begun.

In the struggle that followed, some of the losers also lost their lives. Others merely were removed from power, for there was no one of them who had either Stalin's cunning or his total disregard for human life. Eventually Nikita Khrushchev became dictator. He would never gain Stalin's total power, and within a few years he too would be removed from office. But before that, in 1956, he would make a speech before the Twentieth Congress of the Communist party.

It was the first time that any man in Russia dared speak aloud about Stalin's crimes. Khrushchev told of Stalin's troubles with Lenin and of Lenin's Testament in which he had asked that Stalin be removed from power. He revealed that it was Stalin who had ordered the bloody purges, the tortures, and murders.

Many of the top Communist officials who listened to Khrushchev's speech already knew the secrets he was exposing. They too had served under Stalin. But they dared not explain to the Russian people why, knowing about Stalin's crimes, they had kept silent and carried out his orders. For this reason Khrushchev's speech has never been officially published in Russia.

Long lines of patient Russians still wind through Red Square to visit the tomb near the Kremlin wall which now holds only the remains of Lenin.

Gradually, however, the Russian people began to learn the truth. One by one the great statues that had been raised in Stalin's honor came crashing down. The little statues and the pictures that had adorned the walls of homes and offices disappeared. The cities and schools, the powerhouses and factories that had been named after Stalin, changed their names once more. Finally the government itself had Stalin's body removed from the great mausoleum where it had been placed alongside that of Lenin.

A Russian poet, named Yevtushenko, wrote about the removal of the body:

> *We carried him away—*
> *threw him out of the mausoleum,*
> *But how shall we remove Stalin*
> *from within Stalin's heirs?* . . .
> *As long as the heirs of Stalin*
> *remain on this earth,*
> *I shall feel that Stalin is still there*
> *in the mausoleum.*

And Stalin's heirs, the men who accepted and carried out his orders, are still in power.

It has been said that Joseph Stalin found Russia working with a wooden plow and left it equipped with atomic power. This is true. Under Stalin's rule the Russian people made tremendous industrial progress. But it was progress paid for with blood, terror, and misery far beyond its value.

Chronological List of Events
in Joseph Stalin's Life

1879   Joseph Vissarionovich Djugashvili, later to be known as Joseph Stalin, is born on December 21 in Gori.

1894   Joseph enters the theological seminary in Tiflis to prepare for the priesthood.

1899   In May, Joseph is expelled from the Tiflis seminary. Later that year he works at the Tiflis observatory and becomes active in the underground revolutionary movement.

1901   Joseph helps organize a demonstration of workers in Tiflis. Later that year he moves to Batum and continues his revolutionary activity there.

1902   After riots in Batum, Joseph is arrested for the first time and exiled to Siberia.

1904   Early in the year Joseph escapes from Siberia. In June he marries Ekaterina Svanidze.

1905   Police open fire on workers who are peacefully petitioning the tsar on January 22. Strikes and uprisings spread throughout Russia in the Revolution of 1905.

1907   Ekaterina Svanidze dies in the spring. In June the Tiflis expropriation takes place. During the next few years, Joseph is arrested, exiled to Siberia, and escapes several times.

1912   Stalin is appointed to the Central Committee of the Bolshevik party.

1914   Stalin is arrested for the last time and sentenced to four years of exile in Siberia.

1914   World War I begins in Europe in August. Russia enters the war as an ally of England and France.

1917   In January Stalin, still in Siberia, is ordered to report for military service. After he is rejected, he is sent to the town of Achinsk.

1917   In March the tsarist government is overthrown. Stalin hurries to Petrograd.

1917   Lenin returns to Petrograd in April.

1917   The Bolsheviks gain control of the government in the October Revolution. Following this event, a civil war breaks out between the Bolshevik, or Red army, and the anti-Bolshevik forces, or White army. For the duration of the Civil War, Stalin builds his personal power and prestige within the Bolshevik party.

1919   In March Stalin marries Nadezhda Alliluieva.

1920   By the end of this year, nearly all the White forces are defeated, leaving the Bolsheviks, or Communists as they are now known, in power.

1922   Stalin becomes the general secretary of the Central Committee of the Communist party.

1924   On January 21 Lenin dies. Stalin gradually eliminates his rivals and, within several years, takes full control of the Soviet government.

1928   Stalin institutes the First Five-Year Plan to improve agricultural and industrial output in the Soviet Union.

1932   Stalin's second wife, Nadezhda Alliluieva, dies in November.

1933   Stalin begins the purge trials which result in the death and deportation of vast numbers of Soviet leaders and others.

1939   Stalin and Joachim von Ribbentrop, Hitler's emissary, conclude a nonaggression pact in August. On September 1 the German army invades Poland, beginning World War II.

1941   On June 22 Germany attacks the Soviet Union.

1943   Stalin, Winston Churchill, and Franklin D. Roosevelt meet at Teheran, Iran in November.

1945   Stalin, Churchill, and Roosevelt meet at Yalta in February.

1945   The Germans surrender in May and the Japanese in August, ending World War II.

1953   Stalin dies on the fifth of March.

1961   Stalin is discredited and his body removed from the Lenin Mausoleum.

Glossary

Bolshevik: a member of the more radical branch of the Russian Social Democratic Workers' party from 1903 to 1917. Later the word began to refer to any member of the Russian Communist party.

bourgeois: a member of the middle class—often a shopkeeper, merchant or businessman—whose political beliefs are usually thought to be influenced by his interest in private property.

bourgeoisie: the middle class which, according to Communist teaching, is opposed to the proletariat or wage-earning class.

capitalism: a system under which the means of production —land, factories, etc.—are mostly privately owned and operated for purposes of making a profit, as in the United States.

Central Committee: the executive committee of the Bolshevik party and, later, of the Communist party.

Cheka: the first secret police organization of the Soviet government. It was later called the G.P.U., the O.G.P.U., or the N.K.V.D. at varying times, but its function remained the same.

communism: a theory which advocates the elimination of private property. According to this theory, all property is owned by the community, and all of the people share both the work and the goods produced. It is also a totalitarian system of government, as in the U.S.S.R. in which the government owns all property and, working through a single party, controls almost completely the economic, cultural, and social life of the nation.

duma: in Russia prior to 1917, a council or official assembly. The legislative body set up by Tsar Nicholas II in 1905 was called the Duma.

general secretary: the chief executive officer of the Bolshevik and, later, the Communist party.

Kremlin: an area in Moscow, enclosed by high walls, in which many of the government buildings are located. The word is also used to mean the Soviet government.

kulak: a well-to-do farmer under the tsars. This class was practically wiped out by the First Five-Year Plan.

Menshevik: a member of the less radical faction of the Russian Social Democratic Workers' party. After the October Revolution, Mensheviks were members of a less radical, socialistic party which opposed the Bolshevik government.

Old Bolshevik: a member of the Communist party who joined the revolutionary movement before 1917.

Politburo: the principal policy-making body of a Communist party. In 1952, the Politburo of the Communist Party of the U.S.S.R. became part of the Presidium of the party, the supreme policy-making body of the Soviet Union.

proletariat: the lowest social or economic class of a community. According to Communist teaching, members of the proletariat are industrial workers who lack their own means of production and, therefore, sell their labor to live.

Provisional Government: a group of men appointed by the Duma to administer the Russian government from the time the tsar was deposed until the Bolsheviks took power in the October Revolution.

socialism: any one of several theories or movements in which the means of producing and distributing goods are owned by the government. Although socialism and communism are similar in theory, they differ considerably in actual practice. Socialist governments usually operate within a democratic framework, as opposed to Communist governments, which are usually totalitarian.

soviet: before the Russian Revolution, a council of any kind. After the revolution, it became a local council with powers of local administration. It might also be a higher council elected by a lower council as part of a pyramid of law-making bodies, culminating in the Supreme Soviet, the U.S.S.R. parliament.

tsar: the name of the emperors of Russia before the revolution. *Czar* is another spelling for *tsar*.

Index